Instant Pot Cookbook

Fast And Healthy Instant Pot Recipes

Quick And Easy Instant Pot Recipe Book

Your Essential Pressure Cooker Meal Recipes

Calendar Publishing

Laurel Stewart

Table of Contents

This Page Has Been Intentionally Left Blank

Flip on to find more good stuff inside

Honestly, just flip on

Come on! Go ahead and get those absolutely delish recipes!

Introduction

The Instant Pot has taken the world by storm and it is quickly becoming one of the most popular kitchen appliances on the market.

But what is the Instant Pot and what makes it so special?

The Instant Pot is an electric pressure cooker that enables you to prepare healthy and flavorful meals in a fraction of the time conventional cooking methods would take. Electric pressure cooking turns tough, inexpensive cuts of meat into delectable dishes and it takes the guesswork out of preparing multi-serving meals like soups, stews, and more. All you have to do is add the ingredients and press a button!

As amazing as the Instant Pot is, it does take some getting used to. If you've never used one before, you might be overwhelmed by all of the buttons and the different settings. That's where this book comes into play. Here you'll learn everything you need to become a pro at using the Instant Pot electric pressure cooker.

Now, what can you expect to find in this book?

First and foremost, this book will become your guide to getting started with the Instant Pot quickly. You'll learn how to unbox and assemble your Instant Pot in addition to learning how to clean it and perform a water test before using it the first time. We'll also cover all of the different buttons and pre-set options, so you know how to use the Instant Pot whether you have a recipe or not. Once you've become familiar with the Instant Pot and its parts and settings, we'll quickly review some common mistakes that new users make, and we'll talk about potential problems and their solutions.

By the time you finish this book, you'll have all of the knowledge you need to use your Instant Pot for everything from soups and stews to porridge, poultry, and more!

If you are new to cooking, this book will provide you with the step-by-step instructions you need to prepare all of your favorite meals from scratch. If you're already an accomplished cook, this book will introduce you to a versatile new kitchen appliance that will change the way you cook for yourself and your family.

So, if you're ready to set up your Instant Pot and get cooking, don't delay a moment longer – turn the page and keep reading!

Part 1: Know Your Instant Pot

You don't have to be a master chef to understand the basics of cooking. You prepare your ingredients, you assemble the necessary equipment, and you follow the steps outlined in the recipe. It sounds simple, right?

Unfortunately, cooking is not always as easy as chefs on the Cooking Channel make it seem. In order to follow a recipe, you need to understand the difference between words like "sauté" and "simmer." You need to know what it means when an ingredient has been browned or what it means to steam a vegetable versus frying it. If you don't know these words, even the simplest of recipes can easily become complicated.

If you like the idea of preparing a healthy, home-cooked meal for your family but you are a little bit lacking in cooking skills, the Instant Pot may be just what you need. This device takes the guesswork out of cooking. All you have to do is prepare your ingredients and punch the right buttons – the device does the rest for you!

But what exactly is the Instant Pot?

The Instant Pot is an electric pressure cooker. A pressure cooker is a device that uses water or another cooking liquid inside a sealed vessel to cook food under pressure at a faster rate than it would cook normally. With a pressure cooker, you can turn even the toughest cuts of meat into tender, delicious entrees in under an hour.

Pressure cookers have come a long way over the years. The first pressure cooker was the steam digester, a device invented by French physicist Denis Papin in 1679. His device used steam pressure to increase the boiling point of water, allowing the food inside the vessel to cook more quickly. After presenting it to the Royal Society of London, Papin was admitted to the society but his invention was treated as an object of scientific study rather than a device with any practical application.

It wasn't until the mid- to late-1800s when pressure cookers were manufactured and made available to the common man. Georg Gutbrod of Stuttgart started making pressure cookers from tinned cast iron. In the early 1900s, Jose Alix Martinez from Zaragoza was granted a patent for the pressure cooker – he called it the "express cooking pot." In 1924, he released a book of 360 recipes for the device.

Pressure cookers of this type are known as "old type" pressure cookers and they were made with a weight-modified valve that releases pressure while the device is being used. This type of pressure cooker only offered a single pressure level, though later models allowed the user to change the weight of the valve and, in doing so, change the pressure. Second generation pressure cookers operate with a spring-loaded valve instead – one that is hidden inside a proprietary mechanism. These pressure cookers allowed for two or more pressure settings.

In today's day and age, we enjoy the modern pressure cooker – the electric pressure cooker. Unlike stovetop models from the first and second generation, electric pressure cookers are made with an electric heat source and they are automatically regulated to maintain the desired operating pressure. These pressure cookers also feature spring-loaded valves and integrated timers. The Instant Pot is an electric pressure cooker.

The Instant Pot is an amazing device and it makes pressure cooking accessible to the average person. You don't need a great deal of cooking knowledge to operate the Instant Pot – you simply need to be able to follow a recipe that has been optimized for this method of cooking.

So, what are the benefits of pressure cooking? Why should you consider adding an Instant Pot to your repertoire of kitchen appliances? Here are a few reasons:

- Cooking time can be reduced by as much as 70% which reduces the total preparation time as well.
- Shorter cook times mean that the ingredients retain more of their natural taste and nutritional value.
- Pressure cooking with a single device is more energy-efficient than using multiple pots and pans on different burners.
- Using an electric pressure cooker to prepare the entire meal reduces cleanup – you simply have to clean the one pot.
- Electric pressure cookers can be used to replace a variety of other kitchen appliances including slow cookers, rice cookers, steamers, canners, and more.
- Pressure cookers turn inexpensive, tough cuts of meat (and other foods) into delicious and enjoyable meals.

If these reasons aren't enough to convince you, all that is left is to try the Instant Pot for yourself. In the first section of this book, we'll go over the details of the Instant Pot electric pressure cooker to ensure that you know how to use it properly. We'll talk about all of the different parts, the buttons, and the additional tools and equipment we recommend. Once you've become acquainted with your Instant Pot, we'll get into the recipes – over 100 of them in eight different categories.

So, what are you waiting for? Turn the page and keep reading to learn more about the Instant Pot and what it can do for you!

Chapter 1: What Does The Instant Pot Consist Of?

Now that you have a better idea what the Instant Pot is and what it can do, you may be wondering what it looks like. If you've ever used a slow cooker or rice cooker, the appearance of the Instant Pot may be familiar to you. It is a stand-alone kitchen device that sits on your counter and plugs into the wall.

But what are the different parts, and what do each of them do?

Here is a quick overview of the different parts that come with the Instant Pot. Keep in mind that there are many different models to choose from and each one is slightly unique. <u>That being said, here are some of the parts you'll find</u>:

1. Outer Body – The outer body of the Instant Pot can also be called the housing because it houses the electronic components. In a way, the outer body is the "brain" of the Instant Pot because it includes the display panel you use to control the device's function. It is the outer body of the machine that actually heats up when you turn it on but you have to use the stainless steel inner pot to contain the ingredients.

When you look at the display panel on the Instant Pot, you'll find several things. In the center is a large digital display and a set of buttons you can use to select low pressure or high pressure – you can also choose from three options to change the pressure to "less," "normal," or "more" by using the plus and minus buttons. Surrounding the digital display is an array of one-touch settings:

- Soup
- Meat/Stew
- Bean/Chili
- Poultry

- Rice
- Multigrain
- Porridge
- Steam

When using your Instant Pot, you'll select from these buttons according to the type of food you are cooking. These buttons make it possible for you to cook without a recipe, though you may also use these buttons when following a recipe. Each button is correlated with a different pressure setting and cook time (you can find the specific details in your user manual).

In addition to these buttons there are two rows of other settings you can use to put your Instant Pot to use for applications other than pressure cooking such as slow cooking, sautéing, and making yogurt. There are also buttons for adjusting the pressure and the cook time as well as a Keep Warm/Cancel button.

2. Stainless Steel Inner Pot – This is the part of the Instant Pot where you place your ingredients – never place anything other than the stainless steel inner pot into the body of your Instant Pot. This pot is constructed from high-strength stainless steel, though you can also purchase a nonstick inner pot if you like. This pot can be removed for cleaning or you can place it directly in the refrigerator (with the glass lid) for storing leftovers or if you prepare your ingredients ahead of time.

3. Silicone Sealing Ring – The silicone sealing ring is very important to the function of your Instant Pot. This silicone gasket fits around the lid and it helps to seal steam inside the inner pot so the pressure cooker can do its job. One thing to be mindful of is that the silicone materials can sometimes absorb the odor of strongly scented foods like onions or garlic. For this reason, you might think about buying several extra silicone rings, so you can use them for specific dishes without affecting the flavor. When washing the inner pot after using it, you should also wash the silicone sealing ring.

4. Lid – The lid goes directly on top of the inner pot, working together with the silicone sealing ring to seal in steam. You'll need to use this plastic lid to lock it in place before you are able to turn on the Instant Pot and select a function. Whether or not the lid is detachable depends on the model you choose. For those with detachable covers, you will find that the plastic holders by the side of the pot become handy holders for the cover.

5. Plastic Housing/Pot Handle – This part of the device fits over the glass lid and it houses the pressure release valve and the steam exhaust valve. It also functions as the pot handle, allowing you to open and close the Instant Pot without touching any of the hot parts. The actual shape and size of the plastic housing varies from one model to another and some will have the pressure valve hidden.

6. Float Valve – Inside the plastic housing there is a metal valve that indicates whether the electric pressure cooker is pressurized or not. When the cooker reaches the desired pressure, the valve will pop up – it will drop back down when the pressure has been released. Depending what model you purchase, this valve may or may not be visible – in some models it is hidden under the plastic cover.

7. Steam Exhaust Valve – Also located on the plastic housing lid, the steam valve is what makes it possible for the Instant Pot to build and release pressure. The valve has two positions – one for sealing (locked) and one for venting (open). When you are using the Instant Pot, the steam exhaust valve must be in the sealing (locked) position or the device won't build pressure. If you are using the slow cooking function of the Instant Pot, however, you'll need to set it to the venting (open) position.

8. Pressure Release Knob – You need this to control the Steam Exhaust Valve for its locked as well as venting functions. Take careful note here, my take is always use a long handled spoon or ladle to toggle this knob, as you do not want to be scalded by the hot steam when you push it to the venting position for situations when you need a quick vent.

9. Condensation Collector – This part consists of a small plastic cup that clips to the outer body of the Instant Pot and it collects condensation that is released during slow cooking. You can only use the slow cooking function with the device vented, so some steam will naturally condense and be collected in this plastic cup. This part is not needed when you are using any of the pressure cooking features.

10. Steamer Rack – The final part that comes with the Instant Pot is a stainless-steel steamer rack. You place the rack inside the inner pot to keep food ingredients above the liquid level for steaming rather than braising or boiling.

11. Measuring Cup – Though not technically part of the Instant Pot itself, this electric pressure cooker comes with a measuring cup you can use when preparing meals. It is important to note that the included measuring cup is a 6-ounce cup, not a standard 8-ounce cup so you might still need to use your own set of measuring cups.

Chapter 2: What Other Tools and Equipment Should You Consider?

The Instant Pot itself is already set up for performing a wide range of cooking functions. All you have to do is add your ingredients and choose the proper setting. In order to follow recipes, however, you may need some additional tools or equipment. Here is what we suggest:

- **Steamer Basket** – Some Instant Pot models come with a stainless-steel steamer basket while others do not. If yours doesn't, consider buying a stainless steel or silicone steamer basket – it may come in handy for vegetables.
- **Glass Lid** – A glass lid allows you to keep an eye on the ingredients while they are cooking, particularly when using the sauté or slow-cook settings. Make sure the lid is made from tempered glass, so it can withstand the heat of the Instant Pot while it is cooking.
- **Silicone Inner Pot Cover** – You won't need a silicone inner pot cover for cooking because the silicone sealing ring keeps the steam in. When it comes to storing leftovers, however, having a silicone inner pot cover to seal the inner pot will save you the hassle of transferring your food to another container for storage.
- **Kitchen Tongs** – These kitchen tools come in a variety of sizes and they are very handy to have around. If you need to add or remove ingredients from your Instant Pot, a pair of kitchen tongs might be easier to use than a spoon or spatula.
- **Wooden Spoons** – If you have a stainless-steel inner pot for your Instant Pot, you may not have to worry about scratching the pot. For the nonstick inner pot, however, you want to be careful what kinds of utensils you use to avoid damage. To make sure you can use the same utensils no matter what inner pot you use, stock up on some high-quality wooden spoons.
- **Thermometer** – The Instant Pot is designed to cook at specific temperatures and pressures according to the button you choose. You may, however, still want to have a kitchen thermometer on hand just to make sure that your food is fully cooked to the proper temperature for safe consumption.
- **Baking Pans** – In most recipes, you'll be preparing food in the inner pot of your Instant Pot. For some recipes, however, you may need additional baking pans – smaller ones that can fit inside your inner pot.
- **Oven Mitts** – When removing the inner pot from the outer housing, it is recommended that you use oven mitts or pot holders to protect your hands from the heat. You can choose whichever option is more comfortable for you.
- **Aluminum Foil** – Though not technically a tool, aluminum foil is a great thing to have on hand when using your Instant Pot. You can use it to cover food or crumple up balls of it to raise an auxiliary baking pan off the bottom of your Instant Pot to prevent damage.

Again, each of these tools and pieces of equipment is optional but you may find them very useful when using your Instant Pot. If you're worried about spending a lot of extra money, try using your Instant Pot with the kitchen tools you already have and then decide if you need to buy any extras.

Chapter 3: Setting Up Your Instant Pot the First Time

Familiarizing yourself with the different parts of your Instant Pot is important. Before you use it to cook your first recipe, however, you need to set it up and do a test run. It won't take long, but there are certain steps you should follow – here they are:

1. Take your Instant Pot out of the box and clean the items individually using warm water and dish soap. Make sure everything is dry before assembling the unit.
2. Place the stainless-steel inner pot inside the outer housing.
3. Attach the power cord at the base of the outer housing.
4. Snap the condensation collection cup in place by sliding it into the back of the outer housing (you should install it even when you aren't slow-cooking just to make sure you don't lose it).
5. Check the plastic housing to make sure that all of the necessary parts are in place before you close and test the Instant Pot.
6. Place the silicon sealing ring in the lid and place the lid on the Instant Pot.
7. Place the plastic housing that contains the lid on top of the outer housing and check to make sure the float valve works by pressing it down.
8. Test the steam exhaust valve by switching it from the sealing to the venting position and back – the float valve should pop up when the unit is pressurized but will be in the down position when it is not.
9. Check the anti-block shield on the underside of the lid – it is next to the float valve and it serves to protect the exhaust valve from food particles during cooking.
10. Close the lid, making sure that the arrow on the lid lines up with the arrow on the outer housing.
11. Turn the lid clockwise until the arrow on the lid lines up with the arrow on the outer housing next to the image of a closed lock – if your Instant Pot is plugged in, you'll hear a chime when the pot is closed and locked.
12. Open the Instant Pot by turning the lid counter-clockwise until the arrow on the lid lines up with the arrow next to the image of an open lock on the base.

By following these steps, you can assemble your Instant Pot and make sure that you have all of the necessary parts. From there, you should perform a water test to make sure the unit works properly before you try to cook with it. Here's how:

1. Make sure your Instant Pot is properly assembled and plugged in.
2. Set the steam release valve in the lid to the "sealing" position.
3. Place the stainless-steel inner pot inside the outer housing and pour in about three cups of water.
4. Close and lock the lid by turning the lid clockwise until the arrow on the lid lines up with the arrow on the base next to the closed lock symbol – you should hear a chime.
5. Press the Steam button on the control panel then press the (-)/(+) button until the display reads 2 – the device is now set to steam for 2 minutes.
6. Wait for the device to come to pressure – the display will read "On" until the desired pressure is reached. When the pot comes to pressure the float valve will pop up and the display will start a 2-minute countdown.
7. Allow the device to count down for the full two minutes – you may notice a plastic smell during this test run, but it should go away and shouldn't happen again.

8. When the two minutes is up, the Instant Pot will beep and automatically switch over to Keep Warm mode – the display will show "L0:00" and begin counting up to let you know how much time has elapsed.
9. Turn off the Instant Pot by pressing the Keep Warm/Cancel button – the display should now read "Off" and the float valve should still be up because the unit is still pressurized.
10. Allow the pressure to vent naturally or use the Quick Release function.
    - To use natural release, simply wait for the float valve to drop back down – this could take anywhere from 10 to 30 minutes depending on the pressure level used during cooking.
    - To use the quick release, switch the steam release valve to the "venting" position and wait for the float valve to drop back down (it is a good idea to use a towel or a pot holder to switch the steam release valve so you don't get burned by hot steam).
11. Once the float valve has dropped back down, open the Instant Pot by turning the lid counter-clockwise until the arrow on the lid lines up with the arrow next to the open lock symbol on the base.

As long as you follow these steps correctly and everything happens according to plan, your Instant Pot should be ready to go! You can empty out the water remaining in the inner pot and clean it then start cooking immediately. Good luck!

Chapter 4: Understanding the Different Buttons and How to Use Them

By now you should have a pretty good idea how your Instant Pot works. When it comes time to actually use it for cooking, however, you may be a little confused about which buttons perform which function unless you review them ahead of time. Here is a quick overview of the different buttons on the Instant Pot display and what each one does:

1. Soup/Broth – This button is what you would use to cook broth, stock, or soup. The Instant Pot will automatically control the pressure depending how much liquid you use to prevent it from boiling too heavily. You have the option to adjust the cook time as needed between 20 and 40 minutes – you can also choose between high and low pressure if you like for some models. When using the Soup/Broth setting, it is important that you do not use the Quick Release function because the ingredients will be foamy, and it could shoot out and burn you. Only use the Natural Release option and wait for the float valve to drop back down.

2. Meat/Stew – This setting is designed for beef, pork, and other cuts of meat as well as meat stews, depending on the amount of cooking liquid you use. It defaults to high pressure for 35 minutes, though longer cooking will result in fall-off-the-bone texture. You can use the (-)/(+) buttons to adjust the cooking pressure as follows:

- Less Mode: high pressure for 20 minutes
- Normal Mode: high pressure for 35 minutes
- More Mode: high pressure for 45 minutes

3. Bean/Chili – This setting is designed to cook beans and bean-heavy recipes such as chili. It defaults to high pressure for 30 minutes but you can use the (-)/(+) buttons to adjust the cooking pressure as follows:

- Less Mode: high pressure for 25 minutes
- Normal Mode: high pressure for 30 minutes
- More Mode: high pressure for 40 minutes

Black beans usually need 10 to 15 minutes and kidney beans need 20 to 25 minutes.

4. Poultry – This setting can be used for chicken and turkey. It defaults to high pressure for 15 minutes but you can use the (-)/(+) buttons to adjust the cooking pressure and time as follows:

- Less Mode: high pressure for 5 minutes
- Normal Mode: high pressure for 15 minutes
- More Mode: high pressure for 30 minutes

5. Rice – With this setting, you can cook tender rice in half the time a conventional rice cooker would take. Using this setting, you can cook white rice, short-grain rice, basmati rice, or jasmine rice in about 4 to 8 minutes using a 1:1 ratio of rice to water. The cooking time automatically adjusts depending how much food you use, and it cooks on low pressure. If you prefer to cook at high pressure, choose Manual mode and set the timer to 3 minutes using a 1:1 ratio of rice to water.

6. Multigrain – This is the setting you would use to cook brown rice or wild rice as well as other grains that take longer to cook than white rice. It defaults to 40 minutes of cooking at pressure but you can use the (-)/(+) buttons to adjust the cooking pressure and time as follows:

- Less Mode: pressure cooking for 20 minutes
- More Mode: 45 minutes of soaking, pressure cooking for 60 minutes

To cook brown rice, you'll need a 1:1.25 ratio of rice to water. For wild rice, use a 1:3 ratio of rice to water and a cook time of 22 to 30 minutes at pressure.

7. Porridge – To make porridge, steel-cut oats, and certain grains this is the setting you would use. It defaults to high pressure for 20 minutes which is the ideal setting for rice porridge (congee) but you can use the (-)/(+) buttons to adjust the cooking pressure and time as follows:

- Less Mode: high pressure for 15 minutes
- More Mode: high pressure for 30 minutes

When using the Porridge setting, it is important that you do not use the Quick Release function because the ingredients will be foamy, and it could shoot out and burn you. Only use the Natural Release option and wait for the float valve to pop up.

8. Steam – This setting can be used to steam vegetables, to cook seafood, or to reheat leftovers – just be sure you use the steam rack to prevent food from sticking to the bottom of the inner pot and burning. To use this setting, add 1 to 2 cups of liquid and place the steamer basket in the inner pot then place your ingredients on top. You can use the (-)/(+) buttons to adjust the cooking time as needed. Frozen vegetables and fresh fish usually need 3 to 5 minutes of cooking.

9. Slow Cook – This is by far one of the most useful functions on the Instant Pot because it opens up a whole new category of recipes you can prepare. Rather than cooking the ingredients at high pressure over a shorter period of time, it cooks them at a lower temperature for longer periods of time. The unit defaults to a 4-hour cook time but you can use the (-)/(+) buttons to adjust the cooking time as needed.

10. Sauté – This is actually one of the functions on your Instant Pot that you are likely to use most often. The Sauté function is similar to cooking in a skillet or frying pan – all you need is a little cooking oil along with the ingredients you want to cook. You can use the (-)/(+) buttons to adjust the cooking temperature as follows:

- Less Mode: 275°F to 302°F
- Normal Mode: 320°F to 349°F
- More Mode: 347°F to 410°F

11. Yogurt – To make homemade yogurt in your Instant Pot, you'll need to use a combination of the Steam and Yogurt functions. Start by pouring your milk into glass containers and place them on top of the steam rack with 1 cup of water in the inner pot. Select the Steam function and set it for 1 minute then use the Natural Release.

Next, wait for the milk to cool below 115°F and add the yogurt starter. Press the Yogurt button and select Normal mode and adjust the time according to your recipe by using the (-)/(+) buttons. The device will read "yogt" on the display when it is done.

12. Cake – Not all Instant Pot models have this setting but if yours does, you can use the device to make cake. The device defaults to high pressure for 40 minutes but you can use the (-)/(+) buttons to adjust the cooking pressure and time as follows:

- Less Mode: high pressure for 25 minutes (lighter, moist cake)
- More Mode: high pressure for 50 minutes (denser cake, cheesecake)

13. Egg - Not all Instant Pot models have this setting but if yours does, you can use the device to make eggs. The pre-set times are intended for extra-large eggs, so you may need to adjust the time for smaller eggs. The device defaults to high pressure for 4 minutes but you can use the (-)/(+) buttons to adjust the pressure and time as follows:

- Less Mode: high pressure for 3 minutes (soft-boiled)
- More Mode: high pressure for 5 minutes (hard-boiled)

When using the egg function, it is recommended that you perform a quick release after cooking then transfer the eggs to an ice bath for 5 minutes before peeling.

14. Sterilize – Not all Instant Pot models have this setting but if yours does, you can use the device to pasteurize dairy products or to sterilize utensils. The device defaults to low pressure at 230°F (110°C) which can be used to sterilize utensils not used for meat canning. Less mode is no-pressure sterilization at 181°F (83°C) which is ideal for pasteurizing dairy products. More mode is for high pressure at 239°F (115°C) which is good for sterilizing utensils not intended for meat canning.

In addition to knowing what the preset options on your Instant Pot do, you should also know how to use the other buttons. In fact, some say that the following buttons are the most important to know – here's how to use them:

1. Manual/Pressure – Depending which model of the Instant Pot you have, it may have a Manual or a Pressure button. This is the button you use when you want to manually input the cook time and adjust the pressure or cooking temperature. Simply press the Manual/Pressure button then use the (-)/(+) buttons to adjust the cook time.

2. Adjust – When using the Manual/Pressure button to select the cook time, you can then use the Adjust button to adjust the temperature or pressure. Choose from Less, Normal, or More heat for Sauté, Slow-Cooking, or Yogurt. Models that do not have this button may have a "Cooking" button instead.

3. Timer/Delay Start – This button allows you to delay the cooking start time. Simply select the Manual/Pressure or Slow Cook option and, within 10 seconds, press the Timer/Delay Start button. Pressing it once allows you to adjust the hours using the

(-)/(+) buttons and pressing it a second time allows you to adjust the minutes.

4. Keep Warm/Cancel – When the Instant Pot has finished cooking, it will beep and automatically switch to Keep Warm mode. You'll see an "L" on the display panel along with a count-up timer letting you know how long the pot has been keeping your food warm. It is safe to consume food that has been cooked and kept warm at 145°F to 172°F for up to 10 hours on the Keep Warm function. Press the button to cancel cooking or to return to standby mode. If you make a mistake when selecting the cook time or pressure, just press the cancel button to start over.

Chapter 5: Tips for Caring for Your Instant Pot

The Instant Pot is an amazing device, but it can be a little bit tricky to clean unless you take your time and learn how to do it properly. You should give the pot a quick wipe-down before you use it for the first time and wash any removable parts. After cooking, the cleaning process is very different – here's what you should do:

1. Unplug the Instant Pot before you do any cleaning.
2. Remove the inner pot and clean it well with hot water and dish soap.
3. Take the silicone sealing ring out of the lid and clean it well – wipe down the inside of the lid with a damp cloth as well just to remove condensation.
4. Check the small parts in the plastic housing such as the steam release valve and the anti-block shield for food particles.
5. Wipe down the inside of the inner housing with a damp cloth to remove condensation and any sticky residue left behind by spills.
6. Use a damp cloth to wipe around the edges of the inner housing, getting into all of the recesses where liquid and food particles could collect.
7. Let everything air dry and then reassemble the Instant Pot for storage.

Cleaning your Instant Pot shouldn't take you very long, so make sure you take the time to do it after each use – this is the best way to keep your Instant Pot clean and in good repair for as long as possible. If the stainless-steel inner pot becomes discolored over time, you can renew the finish by wiping it with vinegar.

Chapter 6: Troubleshooting Common Problems with the Instant Pot

When using your Instant Pot for the first time, you should follow the instructions in your recipe very carefully to avoid mistakes. Even if you are careful, however, mistakes do happen, and you should correct them as soon as possible. To get you started on the right foot, here is a quick list of the top 10 problems new Instant Pot users make – read through this list so you can avoid making these same mistakes:

1. Forgetting to place the inner pot inside the outer housing before adding your cooking ingredients.
2. Filling the inner pot above the recommended line.
3. Using the Quick Release method instead of the Natural Release when the pot is very full or the ingredients are foamy.
4. Pressing the Timer button to set the cook time instead of using the (-)/(+) buttons.
5. Forgetting to switch the steam release valve to the venting or sealing position.
6. Adding too much liquid to the inner pot before turning it on.
7. Not using enough liquid when using the Instant Pot for pressure cooking.
8. Forgetting to replace the silicone sealing ring after cleaning it before using.
9. Using the Rice button to cook different types of rice and grains (use the multigrain button instead).
10. Using hot liquid in a recipe that calls specifically for cold liquid.

In addition to familiarizing yourself with some of the most common mistakes new Instant Pot users make, you should also take the time to learn how to troubleshoot different problems. Even once you get the hang of using your Instant Pot, you may run into snags from time to time.

Here are some of the most common problems that happen with the Instant Pot and how to solve them:

1. The Instant Pot is not sealing properly.

While the Instant Pot comes to pressure, you will hear hissing sounds and you may notice some steam coming out of the float valve or steam release handle. As long as the steam release handle is in the "sealing" position, however, the float valve should rise when the device reaches pressure and you should notice little to no steam coming out after that point.

If the Instant Pot doesn't seem to be sealing properly, make sure the silicone sealing ring is in place. Failing that, check to make sure there is enough liquid in the pot for it to come to pressure. Another potential problem that could keep the device from sealing properly is a dirty float valve or anti-block shield – look under the lid to make sure these things are clean.

2. The Instant Pot is making a ticking or cracking sound.

It is normal for the device to make a ticking or light cracking sound when the power is turned on or when the device is changing temperature. Another possible reason is that the bottom of the inner pot is wet – take it out and wipe it down then replace it to see if that solves the problem.

3. The lid on the Instant Pot is not closing or latching properly.

Check to make sure that the silicone sealing ring is installed correctly – it should be tightly in place before you close the lid. If the silicone sealing ring is fine, check the float valve – it should be in the down position when you close the lid.

4. The lid on the Instant Pot will not open or is difficult to open.

If the Instant Pot will not open, it may be because the device is still at pressure – switch the steam release handle to the "venting" position to release pressure or wait for the pressure to vent naturally. If the float valve remains stuck in the popped-up position, try pressing it lightly with a long utensil to loosen it.

5. The Instant Pot is taking longer than usual to reach pressure.

If you find that your Instant Pot is taking longer than normal to reach the desired pressure, there are several things that could be happening. One possible reason is that you are cooking with frozen food – because frozen food takes longer to cook, it will also take longer for the pot to come to pressure. Another reason could be that you have too much liquid in the pot or that you're using more liquid than usual.

6. The Instant Pot isn't working the same as usual at higher altitudes.

You may already be aware that cooking at high altitude comes with certain challenges. When using your Instant Pot at a higher altitude than normal, you may need to add 5% cook time for every 1,000 feet above sea level. If you live at high altitude, you'll get used to this eventually and it will become second nature.

7. The Instant Pot is over-heating or food is burning inside.

In order to prevent overheating and burning, you need to use a minimum of ½ cup of liquid, though you would be safer with 1 ½ to 2 cups of liquid. Keep in mind that some foods release liquid on their own so you can reduce the amount of liquid you use for high-moisture vegetables and similar ingredients.

8. When using low-fat cuts of meat in the Instant Pot, they turn out dry and rubbery.

Pressure cooking is an excellent cooking method for tougher, more inexpensive cuts of meat but lean cuts of meat may cook too quickly for the Instant Pot. Examples of cuts that don't tend to fare well in pressure cooking include beef sirloin, chicken breast, and pork tenderloin. If you do use leaner cuts, cook them in liquid and use the Quick Release venting method to keep them from drying out.

9. I'm not sure whether to use the Quick Release or Natural Release option.

There are two ways to release pressure after your food is cooked – Quick Release or Natural Release. The Natural Release option takes 5 to 30 minutes and it is the best option to use if the ingredients in the Instant Pot may be foamy – this is true for soups and when making oatmeal. It may also be best for large cuts of meat because letting the meat rest after cooking will help seal in the juices.

A Quick Release stops the cooking more quickly than a Natural Release and it is the option to use if you're cooking something that is prone to overcooking – examples would include vegetables and fish or seafood. If you aren't sure which method is best, you can always allow the Instant Pot to vent naturally for 10 minutes and then switch to the Quick Release to vent any remaining steam.

Part 2: Instant Pot Recipes

Now that you've learned the basics about your Instant Pot and how to use it, you're probably eager to give it a go!

The Instant Pot is one of the most versatile kitchen appliances out there, and I'm positive that you are going to love it. Not only does it do the work of half a dozen appliances in one, but it is very easy to use! Sure, it might take some practice to get the hang of using the preset buttons but after a few recipes, you're going to be hooked.

Never again will you have to spend the entire day slaving away to prepare a fresh, healthy meal for your family. With the Instant Pot, you can go from preparation to finished product in under an hour!

So, what can you look forward to in this second part of the book?

The recipes, of course!

In this half of the book, you'll find a large collection of delicious Instant Pot recipes for breakfast, lunch, dinner, and dessert. Each of these recipes requires relatively little preparation and most or all of the cooking happens right in your Instant Pot.

I also want to give you all an idea on how the terms in this book function:

- Prep time – essentially the time you need to prepare the ingredients
- Cook time – the time spent allowing the pot to actually cook the food
- In the Pot time – this not only includes the actual cook time, but the time needed to allow for venting of steam either naturally or by valve release
- Total time – this is the approximate total time with which to prepare and have your meal ready to eat!

So, if you're ready to see how the Instant Pot works, simply pick a recipe and give it a try – you won't be disappointed!

Breakfast Recipes

Recipes Included in this Chapter:

- Mexican-Style Egg Casserole
- Vanilla Steel Cut Oats
- Blueberry French Toast Casserole
- Cheesy Ham and Egg Casserole
- Peaches and Cream Oatmeal
- Cheesy Breakfast Hash
- Easy Cheesy Egg and Veggie Bake
- Butternut Squash Breakfast Porridge
- Chunky Sausage Gravy
- Cheddar Bacon Ranch Breakfast Potatoes
- Cinnamon Baked Apples
- Blueberry Raisin Quinoa Breakfast Bowl
- Giant Western Omelet
- Banana Walnut Steel Cut Oats

Mexican-Style Egg Casserole

Yield: makes 8 servings

Prep Time: 5 minutes

Cook Time: 26 minutes

In the Pot Time: 45 minutes

Total Time: 50 minutes

Function Buttons: Sauté, Manual

Ingredients:

- 1 pound ground pork sausage
- ½ large yellow onion, chopped
- 8 large eggs
- ½ cup all-purpose flour
- 1 medium red pepper, chopped
- 4 green onions, sliced thin
- 1 (15-ounce) can black beans, rinsed and drained
- 1 ¼ cup shredded Mexican blend cheese
- ¾ cup crumbled Cotija cheese

Instructions:

1. Press the Sauté button on the Instant Pot and wait for the display to read "hot."
2. Add the sausage and onion to the pot and cook until the sausage is browned, stirring to break it up into pieces with a wooden spoon, about 6 minutes.

3. Meanwhile, whisk the flour and eggs together in a small bowl then pour it into the pot once the sausage is browned.
4. Stir in the chopped peppers and green onion along with the black beans, Mexican cheese, and Cotija cheese.
5. Close the lid and lock it in place then pressure the Manual button and set the timer to 20 minutes.
6. When the timer runs out, allow the pressure to vent naturally.
7. When the float valve drops back down, unlock and open the lid then transfer the cooked omelet to a serving plate.
8. Let the omelet rest for 5 minutes then cut into slices to serve.

Nutrition: 420 calories per serving, 26.4g fat, 25.1g protein, 19.2g carbs, 3g fiber

Vanilla Steel Cut Oats

Yield: makes 4 servings

Prep Time: 5 minutes

Cook Time: 10 minutes

In the Pot Time: 40 minutes

Total Time: 45 minutes

Function Buttons: Manual

Ingredients:

- 2 ½ cups water
- 1 cup unsweetened vanilla almond milk
- 1 cup steel-cut oats
- 2 to 3 tablespoons sugar
- 1 teaspoon espresso powder
- ¼ teaspoon salt
- ½ tablespoon vanilla extract

Instructions:

1. Whisk together the water, almond milk, steel-cut oats, sugar, espresso and salt in the Instant Pot.
2. Close the lid and lock it in place.
3. Press the Manual button and set the timer to 10 minutes.
4. When the timer goes off, allow the pressure to vent naturally for 10 minutes then press the Cancel button and switch the steam release valve to the "venting" position.
5. When the float valve drops back down, open the lid and stir in the vanilla extract.
6. Close the lid again and let the oats thicken for 5 minutes.
7. Spoon into bowls and serve with a drizzle of cream.

Nutrition: 210 calories per serving, 3.8g fat, 7.3g protein, 35.8g carbs, 5.3g fiber

Blueberry French Toast Casserole

Yield: Makes 6 servings

Prep Time: 10 minutes

Cook Time: 15 minutes

In the Pot Time: 40 minutes

Total Time: 50 minutes

Function Buttons: Manual

Ingredients:

- 1 loaf French bread
- 3 large eggs
- 1 cup half-and-half
- ½ cup skim milk
- 1 tablespoon ground cinnamon
- 1 ½ teaspoons vanilla extract
- 1 teaspoon sugar
- 1 cup fresh blueberries
- Pure maple syrup

Instructions:

1. Grease the inner pot of your Instant Pot with cooking spray.
2. Cut the bread into cubes then place them in the Instant Pot.
3. Whisk together the eggs, half-and-half, milk, cinnamon, sugar and vanilla extract in a bowl then pour over the bread cubes.
4. Toss the bread cubes to coat then sprinkle in the blueberries.
5. Close and lock the lid then press the Manual button and set the timer to 15 minutes.
6. When the timer goes off, allow the pressure to vent naturally then press the Cancel button – wait for the float valve to drop back down.
7. Let the casserole sit with the lid closed for 5 minutes then spoon into bowls and drizzle with maple syrup to serve.

Nutrition: 320 calories per serving, 9.9g fat, 11.9g protein, 45.2g carbs, 3.2g fiber

Cheesy Ham and Egg Casserole

Yield: makes 6 servings

Prep Time: 5 minutes

Cook Time: 25 minutes

In the Pot Time: 45 minutes

Total Time: 5 minutes

Function Buttons: Manual

Ingredients:

- 4 medium red skin potatoes, chopped
- 1 small yellow onion, diced
- 1 cup diced ham
- 2 cups shredded cheddar cheese
- 10 large eggs
- 1 cup skim milk
- Salt and pepper

Instructions:

1. Combine the potatoes, ham, onion, and cheese in a glass bowl that will fit into the inner pot of your Instant Pot.
2. Beat the eggs with the milk, salt, and pepper then pour into the bowl.
3. Place the steamer rack in your Instant Pot and pour in 2 cups of water.
4. Cover the bowl with foil and place it on the rack then close and lock the lid.
5. Press the Manual button and set the timer to 25 minutes.
6. When the timer goes off, press the Cancel button and switch the steam release valve to the "venting" position for a Quick Release.
7. Open the lid when the float valve drops back down.
8. Remove the bowl from the Instant Pot and cut the casserole into portions.
9. Serve hot topped with sour cream and avocado, if desired.

Nutrition: 430 calories per serving, 22.9g fat, 27.7g protein, 27.7g carbs, 3g fiber

Peaches and Cream Oatmeal

Yield: makes 8 servings

Prep Time: 5 minutes

Cook Time: 6 minutes

In the Pot Time: 35 minutes

Total Time: 40 minutes

Function Buttons: Porridge

Ingredients:

- 4 large peaches, fresh
- 4 cups old-fashioned oats
- 4 cups water
- 3 cups milk (or almond milk)
- 1 ½ teaspoons ground cinnamon
- 1 teaspoon salt
- ¼ to 1/3 cup white sugar

Instructions:

1. Wash the peaches then peel them and chop them up before adding them to the inner pot of your Instant Pot.
2. Add the old-fashioned oats, water, milk, cinnamon, and salt.
3. Stir in the sugar according to your liking then close and lock the lid.
4. Press the Porridge button and adjust the timer down to 6 minutes.
5. When the timer goes off, allow the pressure to vent naturally for 15 minutes then press the Cancel button.
6. Switch the steam release valve to the "venting" position and wait for the float valve to drop back down.
7. Stir the oatmeal well and adjust the sweetness to taste.
8. Spoon into bowls and serve with brown sugar, cream, and fresh sliced peaches.

Nutrition: 270 calories per serving, 5g fat, 9.6g protein, 48.5g carbs, 5.9g fiber

Cheesy Breakfast Hash

Yield: makes 8 servings

Prep Time: 10 minutes

Cook Time: 20 minutes

In the Pot Time: 50 minutes

Total Time: 1 hour

Function Buttons: Sauté, Manual

Ingredients:

- 1 (12-ounce) package bacon, chopped
- 4 medium red skin potatoes, diced
- 12 large eggs
- ¼ cup milk
- ½ teaspoon salt
- ¼ teaspoon pepper
- 1 cup shredded cheddar cheese
- 3 green onions, sliced thin

Instructions:

1. Press the Sauté button on the Instant Pot and wait for the display to read "hot."
2. Add the bacon to the inner pot and cook until crisp, stirring as needed to keep it from burning.
3. Drain the grease and spread the bacon in the bottom of a spring-form pan sized to fit inside the Instant Pot – sprinkle the potatoes over top.
4. Beat together the eggs, milk, salt, and pepper in a bowl then pour into the spring-form pan and cover with foil
5. Place the steamer insert in the Instant Pot and add 1 cup of water before placing the spring-form pan inside.
6. Close and lock the lid then press the Manual button and adjust the timer to 20 minutes.
7. When the timer goes off, allow the pressure to vent naturally until the float valve sinks back down.

8. Press the Cancel button then unlock and open the Instant Pot.
9. Remove the spring-form pan from the Instant pot then run a knife around the edges to loosen the egg before removing the outer ring.
10. Place the casserole on a serving plate and sprinkle with cheese and green onions.
11. Allow the cheese to melt (place it under the broiler, if needed) then cut into slices and serve hot.

Nutrition: 475 calories per serving, 30.2g fat, 31.1g protein, 19.1g carbs, 2g fiber

Easy Cheesy Egg and Veggie Bake

Yield: makes 6 servings

Prep Time: 10 minutes (including Sauté)

Cook Time: 20 minutes

In the Pot Time: 45 minutes

Total Time: 1 hour

Function Buttons: Sauté, Manual

Ingredients:

- 8 slices bacon, chopped
- 1 small yellow onion, chopped
- 1 small red pepper, chopped
- 1 small green pepper, chopped
- 2 cups frozen hash browns
- 6 large eggs
- ¼ cup skim milk
- ½ cup shredded cheddar cheese
- Salt and pepper

Instructions:

1. Press the Sauté button on the Instant Pot and wait for the display to read "hot."
2. Add the bacon and cook for 2 minutes, stirring occasionally.
3. Stir in the chopped onions and pepper and sauté for 3 minutes until the onions are translucent.
4. Add the frozen hash browns then stir everything together and cook for 2 minutes.
5. Press the Cancel button then grease a heat-proof baking dish or bowl that will fit in your Instant Pot.
6. Spoon the bacon, veggies, and hash browns into the dish.
7. Beat together the eggs, milk, cheese, salt, and pepper then pour it into the dish.
8. Place the steamer insert in your Instant Pot and pout in 1 ½ cups water.
9. Place the dish on the insert then close and lock the lid.
10. Press the Manual button and adjust the timer to 20 minutes.
11. When the timer goes off, press the Cancel button and switch the steam release valve to the "venting" position.
12. When the float valve drops back down, unlock and open the lid then remove the dish and run a knife around the edges to loosen the egg.
13. Turn the egg out onto a serving dish and let rest for 5 minutes before slicing into wedges to serve.

Nutrition: 350 calories per serving, 20.2g fat, 22.2g protein, 19.5g carbs, 1.8g fiber

Butternut Squash Breakfast Porridge

Yield: makes 6 servings

Prep Time: 5 minutes

Cook Time: 8 minutes

In the Pot Time: 35 minutes

Total Time: 40 minutes

Function Buttons: Manual

Ingredients:

- 3 cups butternut squash, cubed
- 4 small ripe apples, peeled and sliced thick
- ½ cup water
- 2 teaspoons ground cinnamon
- 1 teaspoon ground cloves
- 1 teaspoon ground ginger
- 2 tablespoons brown sugar
- 2 tablespoons maple syrup
- Pinch salt

Instructions:

1. Place the butternut squash and apple slices into the Instant Pot.
2. Pour in the water and sprinkle in the cinnamon, cloves, and ginger.
3. Close and lock the lid then press the Manual button and set the timer to 8 minutes.
4. When the timer goes off, allow the pressure to vent naturally for 10 minutes.
5. Press the Cancel button and switch the steam release valve to the "venting" position to release any remaining pressure.
6. When the float valve drops back down, unlock and open the lid and transfer the contents of the Instant Pot to a food processor.
7. Add the brown sugar, maple syrup, and a pinch of salt then blend smooth.
8. Spoon into bowls and serve with a drizzle of cream and some toasted coconut or chopped nuts (optional).

Nutrition: 142 calories per serving, 0.5g fat, 1.5g protein, 37 g carbs, 5.6g fiber

Chunky Sausage Gravy

Yield: makes 6 servings

Prep Time: 5 minutes

Cook Time: 5 minutes

In the Pot Time: 40 minutes

Total Time: 45 minutes

Function Buttons: Sauté (More)

Ingredients:

- 1 pound ground pork sausage
- ½ cup chicken broth
- 3 cups 2% milk
- ½ cup all-purpose flour
- Salt and pepper

Instructions:

1. Press the Sauté button and adjust it to the More setting.
2. When the display panel reads "hot," add the sausage and cook until browned, breaking it up with a spoon.
3. Pour in the chicken broth then close and lock the lid.
4. Press the Manual button and adjust the timer to 5 minutes.
5. When the timer goes off, press the Cancel button and switch the steam release valve to the "venting" position.
6. Wait for the float valve to drop back down while you whisk the milk together with the flour until no lumps remain.
7. Unlock and open the lid then pour the milk mixture into the Instant Pot.
8. Press the Sauté button and adjust it to More then season the contents with salt and pepper.
9. Cook until the sausage gravy is thick and bubbling, stirring occasionally, then serve over fresh biscuits.

Nutrition: 305 calories per serving, 18.6g fat, 17g protein, 15.8g carbs, 0.3g fiber

Cheddar Bacon Ranch Breakfast Potatoes

Yield: makes 6 servings

Prep Time: 10 minutes

Cook Time: 7 minutes

In the Pot Time: 30 minutes

Total Time: 40 minutes

Function Buttons: Sauté, Manual

Ingredients:

- 4 slices bacon, chopped
- 2 pounds red skin potatoes, cut into 1-inch chunks
- 2 teaspoons dried parsley
- 1 teaspoon garlic powder
- ½ teaspoon onion powder
- Salt and pepper, to taste
- 1/3 cup water
- 4 to 6 tablespoons ranch dressing
- 1 cup shredded cheddar cheese

Instructions:

1. Press the Sauté button on your Instant Pot and wait for the display panel to read "hot."
2. Add the bacon and cook until crisp, stirring as needed to keep it from burning – about 2 to 3 minutes.
3. Stir in the potatoes, parsley, garlic powder, and onion powder then season with salt and pepper.
4. Pour in the water the close and lock the lid.
5. Press the Manual button and adjust the timer to 7 minutes.
6. When the timer goes off, press the Cancel button and switch the steam release valve to the "venting" position.
7. When the float valve drops back down, unlock and open the lid then stir in the ranch dressing and cheddar cheese.
8. Once the cheese is melted, adjust seasoning to taste and serve hot.

Nutrition: 265 calories per serving, 13.8g fat, 10g protein, 25.4g carbs, 2.7g fiber

Cinnamon Baked Apples

Yield: makes 6 servings

Prep Time: 5 minutes

Cook Time: 8 minutes

In the Pot Time: 30 minutes

Total Time: 35 minutes

Function Buttons: Manual

Ingredients:

- 6 medium apples
- 1 1/2 cups unsweetened apple juice
- ¼ to ½ cup white sugar or brown sugar
- 2 tablespoons ground cinnamon
- 1 cup granola (optional)
- 1/4 cup Heavy cream (optional)

Instructions:

1. Wash the apples then carefully remove the cores, keeping the apples whole.
2. Place the apples in the Instant Pot in a single layer and pour in the apple juice.
3. Sprinkle with sugar and cinnamon then close and lock the lid.
4. Press the Manual button and adjust the timer to 8 minutes.
5. When the timer goes off, allow the steam to vent naturally for 10 minutes then press the Cancel button.
6. Switch the steam release valve to the "venting" position and wait for the float valve to drop back down.
7. Unlock and open the lid then spoon the apples into bowls.
8. Sprinkle with granola then drizzle with milk or cream to serve.

Nutrition: 245 calories per serving (with granola), 2.7g fat, 2.5g protein, 58.1g carbs, 7.8g fiber

Blueberry Raisin Quinoa Breakfast Bowl

Yield: makes 4 servings

Prep Time: 5 minutes

Cook Time: 1 minute

In the Pot Time: 25 minutes

Total Time: 30 minutes

Function Buttons: Manual

Ingredients:

- 1 ½ cups uncooked quinoa
- 1 ½ cups unsweetened almond milk
- 1 cinnamon stick
- 1 cup fresh blueberries
- ¼ cup seedless raisins
- ¼ cup sliced almonds
- ½ cup plain nonfat Greek yogurt

Instructions:

1. Rinse the quinoa well then place it in the Instant Pot.
2. Stir in the almond milk and add the cinnamon stick then close and lock the lid.
3. Press the Manual button and set the timer to 1 minute.
4. When the timer goes off, allow the pressure to vent naturally for 10 minutes then press the Cancel button and switch the steam release valve to the "venting" position.
5. When the float valve drops back down, unlock and open the lid and spoon the quinoa into a bowl, discarding the cinnamon stick.
6. Stir in the blueberries, raisins, and almonds.
7. Spoon into bowls and top with a dollop of yogurt to serve.

Nutrition: 320 calories per serving, 5.3g fat, 13.8g protein, 55.1g carbs, 6.1g fiber

Giant Western Omelet

Yield: makes 4 servings

Prep Time: 10 minutes

Cook Time: 30 minutes

In the Pot Time: 50 minutes

Total Time: 1 hour

Function Buttons: Manual

Ingredients:

- 6 large eggs
- ½ cup milk
- Salt and pepper

- 8 ounces diced ham
- ½ cup diced red pepper
- ¼ cup diced green pepper
- 1 small yellow onion, diced
- 1 cup shredded cheddar cheese

Instructions:

1. Place the steamer insert in the Instant Pot and pour in 1 ½ cups of water.
2. Find a souffle dish that will fit in the Instant Pot and grease it with cooking spray.
3. Beat together the eggs, milk, salt and pepper in a bowl then pour into the dish.
4. Stir in the ham, peppers, onions, and cheese then cover the dish loosely with foil.
5. Close and lock the lid then press the Manual button and adjust the timer to 30 minutes.
6. When the timer goes off, let the pressure vent naturally for 10 minutes then hit the Cancel button.
7. Switch the steam release valve to the "venting" position and wait for the float valve to drop back down.
8. Unlock and open the lid then lift out the souffle dish.
9. Let the omelet set for 5 minutes then slice into wedges to serve.

Nutrition: 340 calories per serving, 22.4g fat, 27.3g protein, 7.7g carbs, 1.4g fiber

Banana Walnut Steel Cut Oats

Yield: makes 4 servings

Prep Time: 5 minutes

Cook Time: 10 minutes

In the Pot Time: 30 minutes

Total Time: 40 minutes

Function Buttons: Manual

Ingredients:

- 2 cups water
- 1 cup unsweetened vanilla almond milk
- 1 cup steel cut oats
- 1/3 cup finely chopped walnuts
- 2 tablespoons ground flaxseed
- 2 tablespoons chia seeds
- 2 tablespoons honey
- 1 ¼ teaspoon ground cinnamon
- 1 teaspoon vanilla extract
- Pinch salt
- 1 large banana, very ripe

Instructions:

1. Combine the water, almond milk, steel cut oats, and walnuts in the Instant Pot.
2. Stir in the flaxseed, chia seeds, honey, cinnamon, vanilla, and salt.
3. Mash the banana in a small bowl then fold it into the ingredients in the Instant Pot.

4. Close and lock the lid then press the Manual button and adjust the timer to 10 minutes.
5. When the timer goes off, press the Cancel button and switch the steam release valve to the "venting" position.
6. When the float valve drops back down, unlock and open the lid.
7. Spoon the oatmeal into bowls and serve with banana slices and drizzled cream.

Nutrition: 285 calories per serving, 12.9g fat, 8.4g protein, 37.5g carbs, 8.8g fiber

Appetizer Recipes

Recipes Included in this Chapter:

- Honey Glazed Chicken Wings
- Sweet and Spicy Meatballs
- Sweet Pulled Pork Sliders
- Spinach Artichoke Dip
- Sweet and Smokey Cocktail Sausages
- Cheesy Pizza Dip
- Brisket Sliders with Caramelized Onions
- Creamy Black Bean Dip
- Easy Avocado Devilled Eggs
- Cranberry Almond Baked Brie
- Prosciutto-Wrapped Asparagus
- Lemon Garlic Hummus

Honey Glazed Chicken Wings

Yield: 4 servings

Prep Time: 5 minutes (plus 20 minutes marinating)

Cook Time: 5 minutes

In the Pot Time: 30 minutes

Total Time: 1 hour

Function Buttons: Sauté, Manual

Ingredients:

- ¼ cup soy sauce
- 1 tablespoon rice wine
- 1 teaspoon sugar
- ¼ teaspoon salt (more to taste)
- 2 pounds chicken wings
- 1 tablespoon coconut oil
- 1 small shallot minced
- 1 tablespoon fresh ginger, sliced thin
- 1 tablespoon minced garlic
- ½ cu p warm water
- 2 tablespoons honey

Instructions:

1. Whisk together the soy sauce, rice wine, sugar, and salt in a shallow dish.
2. Add the chicken wings and toss to coat then cover and chill for 20 minutes.
3. Press the Sauté button to preheat the Instant Pot and press the More button to adjust the temperature – wait for the display panel to read "hot."

4. Add the coconut oil to the Instant Pot and let it melt then add the chicken wings, reserving the extra marinade.
5. Cook the chicken wings for 30 seconds then turn and cook for 30 seconds on the other side – remove them to a bowl.
6. Press the Cancel button then the Sauté button again to preheat the Instant Pot to medium (Normal) heat.
7. Add the shallot, ginger, and garlic and cook for 30 seconds.
8. Whisk together the water and honey then pour into the pot and stir to loosen any browned bits.
9. Add the chicken wings and the reserved marinade to the pot.
10. Close the lid and press the Manual button and set the timer for 5 minutes.
11. After the timer goes off, allow the pressure to vent naturally – about 10 minutes – then press the Cancel button.
12. When the float valve drops down, unlock and open the lid.
13. Season the chicken wings with salt to taste and serve hot.

Nutrition: 401 calories per serving, 25.9g fat, 27.5g protein, 10.2g carbs, 0.2g fiber

Sweet and Spicy Meatballs

Yield: 6 (3-meatball) servings

Prep Time: 10 minutes

Cook Time: 25 minutes

In the Pot Time: 25 minutes

Total Time: 1 hour

Function Buttons: Manual

Ingredients:

- 1 pound (85%) lean ground beef
- ½ cup plain breadcrumbs
- 1 large egg
- ¼ cup grated parmesan cheese
- 2 tablespoons fresh chopped parsley
- 2 tablespoons minced white onion
- 1 (12-ounce) jar chili sauce
- 1 (12-ounce) jar grape jelly
- ½ cup warm water
- 1 to 2 teaspoons red pepper flakes

Instructions:

1. Combine the ground beef, breadcrumbs, egg, parmesan cheese, parsley, and minced onion in a mixing bowl.
2. Stir until well combined then shape into 1-inch balls by hand (about 24).
3. Place the meatballs on a baking sheet and broil on high heat for 15 minutes.
4. While the meatballs are cooking, whisk together the chili sauce, grape jelly, water, and red pepper flakes.
5. Transfer the meatballs to the Instant Pot then pour the sauce over them.
6. Press the Manual button and adjust the time to 10 minutes (Normal).

7. After the timer goes off, allow the pressure to vent naturally – about 10 minutes – then press the Cancel button.
8. When the float valve drops down, the Instant Pot will automatically switch to Keep Warm – keep warm until ready to serve.

Nutrition: 335 calories per serving, 6.1g fat, 19.5g protein, 49.7g carbs, 0.9g fiber

Sweet Pulled Pork Sliders

Yield: 16 servings

Prep Time: 10 minutes

Cook Time: 60 minutes

In the Pot Time: 1 hour 25 minutes

Total Time: 1 hour 35 minutes

Function Buttons: Sauté, Manual

Ingredients:

- ½ cup apple cider vinegar
- ½ cup ketchup
- 5 tablespoons brown sugar
- 2 tablespoons molasses
- 1 tablespoon Worcestershire sauce
- 2 tablespoons chili powder
- Salt and pepper
- 1 (5-pound) boneless pork shoulder

Instructions:

1. Whisk together the apple cider vinegar, ketchup, brown sugar, molasses, and Worcestershire sauce in a mixing bowl.
2. Press the Sauté button on the Instant Pot and add the oil – wait for the display panel to read "hot."
3. Season the pork shoulder with chili powder, salt, and pepper then place it in the Instant Pot.
4. Cook for 2 to 3 minutes until browned then flip the pork and cook until browned on the other side – another 2 to 3 minutes.
5. Press the Cancel button then pour in the sauce to coat the pork, spreading it over the roast if needed.
6. Close the lid and press the Manual button and set the time for 60 minutes.
7. After the timer goes off, allow the pressure to vent naturally – about 10 minutes – then press the Cancel button.
8. When the float valve drops down, unlock and open the lid.
9. Remove the pork to a cutting board and shred the meat with two forks.
10. Spoon the pork into a serving bowl.
11. Serve on toasted slider buns with barbecue sauce and your choice of toppings.

Nutrition: 395 calories per serving, 28.9g fat, 24g protein, 7.3g carbs, 0.3g fiber

Spinach Artichoke Dip

Yield: 10 servings

Prep Time: 5 minutes

Cook Time: 4 minutes

In the Pot Time: 10 minutes

Total Time: 15 minutes

Function Buttons: Manual

Ingredients:

- 1 (14-ounce) can artichoke hearts, drained and chopped
- 1 (10-ounce) package frozen spinach, thawed
- 1 (8-ounce) package cream cheese, softened
- ½ cup mayonnaise
- 1 tablespoon minced garlic
- ½ cup chicken broth
- 1 teaspoon onion powder
- 2 cups shredded parmesan cheese
- 1 cup shredded mozzarella cheese

Instructions:

1. Combine the artichoke hearts, frozen spinach, cream cheese, mayonnaise, and garlic in the Instant Pot.
2. Stir together the chicken broth and onion powder then pour into the pot.
3. Close the Instant Pot and press the Manual button and set the time for 4 minutes.
4. When the timer goes off, perform a Quick Release by switching the steam release valve to the "venting" position.
5. When the float valve drops down, unlock and open the lid.
6. Stir in the parmesan cheese and mozzarella cheese and wait for it to melt.
7. Spoon the dip into a bowl and serve with crackers or chips for dipping.

Nutrition: 250 calories per serving, 21.5g fat, 11.2g protein, 5.2g carbs, 1.4g fiber

Sweet and Smokey Cocktail Sausages

Yield: makes 8 servings

Prep Time: 5 minutes

Cook Time: 1 minute

In the Pot Time: 10 minutes

Total Time: 15 minutes

Function Buttons: Manual, Sauté, Keep Warm

Ingredients:

- 2 (12-ounce) packages cocktail sausages
- 1 cup barbecue sauce
- ½ cup beer
- ¼ cup brown sugar, packed
- 1 tablespoon apple cider vinegar
- 1 tablespoon honey

Instructions:

1. Place the cocktail sausages in the Instant Pot.
2. Whisk together the barbecue sauce, beer, brown sugar, vinegar, and honey in a bowl then pour over the sausages.
3. Close the Instant Pot and press the Manual button and set the timer for 1 minute.
4. When the timer goes off, press the Cancel button and allow the pressure to vent naturally – about 5 minutes.
5. Press the Sauté button and set the timer for 5 minutes to thicken the sauce.
6. When the timer goes off, the device will automatically switch to Keep Warm – let the Instant Pot keep the sausages warm until you are ready to serve them.

Nutrition: 285 calories per serving, 14.8g fat, 11.9g protein, 25.5g carbs, 1.2g fiber

Cheesy Pizza Dip

Yield: makes 6 servings

Prep Time: 5 minutes

Cook Time: 20 minutes

In the Pot Time: 30 minutes

Total Time: 35 minutes

Function Buttons: Manual

Ingredients:

- 1 (8-ounce) package cream cheese, softened
- ½ cup pizza sauce
- 4 ounces shredded mozzarella cheese
- ½ to 1 teaspoon dried basil

Instructions:

1. Place the steamer insert in your Instant Pot and pour in two cups of water.
2. Spread the cream cheese along the bottom of a 7-cup glass baking dish (one that will fit inside your Instant Pot).
3. Pour the pizza sauce over the cream cheese and spread it evenly.
4. Sprinkle with shredded mozzarella cheese and dried basil.
5. Place the baking dish on the steamer insert in your Instant Pot and close the lid.
6. Press the Manual button and adjust the timer to 20 minutes.
7. When the timer goes off, switch the steam release valve to the "venting" position to Quick Release then press the Cancel button.
8. Once the pressure has vented, open the Instant Pot and remove the baking dish.

9. Cool the pizza dip for a few minutes before serving with chips for dipping.

Nutrition: 200 calories per serving, 16.6g fat, 8.5g protein, 4g carbs, 0.3g fiber

Brisket Sliders with Caramelized Onions

Yield: makes 12 servings

Prep Time: 5 minutes (plus 30 minutes chill time)

Cook Time: 50 minutes

In the Pot Time: 1 hour 15 minutes

Total Time: 1 hour 50 minutes

Function Buttons: Sauté, Manual

Ingredients:

- 2 tablespoons salt
- ½ tablespoon fresh cracked pepper
- 2 teaspoons paprika
- 1 teaspoon cayenne
- 1 teaspoon dried oregano
- 3 pounds boneless beef brisket
- 3 tablespoons olive oil, divided
- 1 tablespoon liquid smoke
- 2 cups beef broth
- 2 medium yellow onions, sliced
- 1 teaspoon sugar

Instructions:

1. Combine the salt, pepper, paprika, cayenne, and oregano in a small bowl.
2. Pat the brisket dry with paper towel then rub generously with the spice mixture.
3. Wrap in plastic then refrigerate for 30 minutes.
4. Turn the Instant Pot to the Sauté setting then add 2 tablespoons olive oil – wait for the display panel to read "hot."
5. Add the brisket to the Instant Pot and cook for 2 to 3 minutes until browned.
6. Turn the brisket and cook to brown on the other side then turn it so the fatty side is facing up.
7. Pour in the liquid smoke and beef broth then close and seal the Instant Pot.
8. Press the Manual button and adjust the timer to 50 minutes.
9. While the brisket is cooking, prepare the sautéed onions on the stovetop.
10. Heat the remaining olive oil in a large skillet over medium-high heat then add the onions and stir to coat with oil.
11. Spread the onions evenly in the skillet and cook on medium heat for 10 minutes, stirring occasionally.
12. Sprinkle with sugar and salt then cook for another 30 minutes, stirring occasionally, until they are caramelized and browned.
13. Reduce the heat to low and keep the onions warm while the brisket finishes cooking.
14. When the timer goes off, allow the pressure to vent naturally – about 10 to 15 minutes – then press the Cancel button to Quick Release the steam.
15. When the float valve drops down, unlock and open the lid.

16. Remove the brisket to a cutting board and shred with two forks then transfer to a serving bowl.
17. Serve the brisket hot with the caramelized onions on toasted slider buns with your favorite barbecue sauce.

Nutrition: 405 calories per serving, 22.3g fat, 11.1g protein, 2.7g carbs, 0.7g fiber

Creamy Black Bean Dip

Yield: makes 24 servings

Prep Time: 5 minutes

Cook Time: 30 minutes

In the Pot Time: 60 minutes

Total Time: 1 hour 5 minutes

Function Buttons: Bean/Chili

Ingredients:

- 1 ½ cups dried black beans (soaked in water overnight)
- 1 (14.5-ounce) can diced tomatoes
- 1 medium yellow onion, diced
- 2 jalapenos, seeded and chopped
- 3 cloves minced garlic
- 1 ¾ cups vegetable broth
- 2 tablespoons olive oil
- 2 tablespoons fresh lime juice
- 1 tablespoon ground cumin
- 1 teaspoon paprika
- 1 teaspoon chili powder
- ½ teaspoon ground coriander
- Salt and pepper

Instructions:

1. Rinse the beans well and drain them then pour them into the Instant Pot.
2. Add our diced tomatoes, onion, jalapeno, and garlic then stir in the vegetable broth, olive oil, and lime juice.
3. Sprinkle in the cumin, paprika, chili powder, coriander, salt, and pepper then stir until well combined.
4. Press the Bean/Chili button – the Instant Pot will automatically cook to 30 minutes at high pressure.
5. When the timer goes off, press the Cancel button and allow the pressure to vent naturally for 10 minutes.
6. Switch the steam release valve to the "venting" position to Quick Release the remaining pressure.
7. When the float valve drops down, unlock and open the lid.
8. Turn off the Instant Pot then use an immersion blender to puree the dip.
9. Adjust the seasoning to taste then serve warm with chips for dipping.

Nutrition: 145 calories per serving, 1.9g fat, 8.5g protein, 24.3g carbs, 6.1g fiber

Easy Avocado Devilled Eggs

Yield: makes 12 (2-piece) servings

Prep Time: 15 minutes (including cooling)

Cook Time: 5 minutes

In the Pot Time: 15 minutes

Total Time: 30 minutes

Function Buttons: Manual

Ingredients:

- 12 large eggs
- 1 medium avocado, pitted and chopped
- ½ cup mayonnaise
- 2 tablespoons fresh lemon juice
- 1 tablespoon Dijon mustard
- Salt and pepper

Instructions:

1. Place the steamer basket in your Instant Pot and pour in 1 cup of water.
2. Add the eggs to the Instant Pot, placing them in the steamer basket.
3. Close the lid to seal the Instant Pot then press the Manual button and set the timer to 5 minutes.
4. When the timer goes off, allow the pressure to vent naturally for 5 minutes then switch the steam release valve to the "venting" position to vent the remaining the pressure.
5. When the float valve drops down, unlock and open the lid.
6. Immediately transfer the eggs to an ice bath to cool for 5 to 10 minutes.
7. When the eggs are cool, peel them and cut them in half.
8. Scoop the yolks into a mixing bowl and stir in the avocado (mashing it as you go) along with the mayonnaise, lemon juice, Dijon mustard, salt and pepper.
9. Spoon the filling back into the egg whites and chill until ready to serve.

Nutrition: 165 calories per serving, 15g fat, 6.7g protein, 2g carbs, 1.2g fiber

Cranberry Almond Baked Brie

Yield: makes 8 (1-ounce) servings

Prep Time: 5 minutes

Cook Time: 15 minutes

In the Pot Time: 25 minutes

Total Time: 30 minutes

Function Buttons: Manual

Ingredients:

- 1 (8-ounce) round of brie
- ¼ cup cranberry preserves
- ¼ cup toasted almonds, chopped

Instructions:

1. Cut slices in the top rind of the brie then place it in a baking dish that will fit inside your Instant Pot and cover tightly with foil.
2. Place the steamer rack in the Instant Pot and pour in 1 cup of water.
3. Set the baking dish on the steamer rack, centering it in the Instant Pot then close and lock the lid.
4. Press the Manual button and adjust the timer to 15 minutes.
5. When the timer goes off, switch the steam release valve to the "venting" position to Quick Release the steam and remove the lid.
6. Remove the dish from the Instant Pot and unwrap it – transfer the brie to a serving plate.
7. Spoon the cranberry preserves and toasted almonds over the brie and serve warm with toasted baguette or crackers for dipping.

Nutrition: 120 calories per serving, 7.5g fat, 5.7g protein, 6.4g carbs, 0.7g fiber

Prosciutto-Wrapped Asparagus

Yield: makes 8 (3-piece) servings

Prep Time: 5 minutes

Cook Time: 2 minutes

In the Pot Time: 15 minutes

Total Time: 20 minutes

Function Buttons: Manual

Ingredients:

- 1 bunch medium asparagus spears (about 24)
- 8 ounces prosciutto, sliced thin
- 2 tablespoons balsamic vinegar

Instructions:

1. Trim the ends from the asparagus and wrap each spear in a piece of prosciutto.
2. Place the steamer basket in the Instant Pot and pour in 2 cups of water.
3. Line the asparagus along the bottom of the steamer basket in a single layer then close and lock the lid.
4. Press the Manual button and set the timer to 2 minutes.
5. When the timer goes off, switch the steam release valve to the "venting" position to Quick Release the pressure.
6. When the float valve drops down, unlock and open the lid.
7. Transfer the asparagus immediately to a serving platter and drizzle with balsamic vinegar to serve.

Nutrition: 50 calories per serving, 1.5g fat, 7g protein, 2.3g carbs, 1g fiber

Lemon Garlic Hummus

Yield: makes 12 servings

Prep Time: 10 minutes (after cooking)

Cook Time: 40 minutes

In the Pot Time: 1 hour

Total Time: 1 hour 10 minutes

Function Buttons: Manual

Ingredients:

- 1 ½ cups dried chickpeas
- 6 cups water
- ½ cup tahini
- 3 to 4 tablespoons fresh lemon juice
- 1 tablespoon minced garlic
- 1 ½ teaspoons salt
- Paprika, to taste
- Fresh chopped parsley

Instructions:

1. Combine the chickpeas and water in the Instant Pot then close and lock the lid.
2. Press the Manual button and adjust the timer to 40 minutes.
3. When the timer goes off, allow the pressure to vent naturally for 15 minutes then switch the steam release valve to the "venting" position to Quick Release the rest of the pressure.
4. When the float valve drops down, unlock and open the lid.
5. Place a colander over a large bowl and pour the chickpeas into it, collecting the cooking liquid in the bowl.
6. Transfer the chickpeas to a food processor then add the tahini, lemon juice, garlic, and salt.
7. Blend until smooth and creamy, adding ¼ up to ¾ cup of the cooking liquid as needed to reach the desired consistency.
8. Adjust the seasoning to taste and spoon into a bowl – sprinkle with paprika and fresh parsley to serve.

Nutrition: 150 calories per serving, 6.9g fat, 6.6g protein, 17.6g carbs, 5.3g fiber

Beans, Grains, and Vegetables

Recipes Included in this Chapter:

- Cilantro Lime Rice
- Wild Rice
- Basic Quinoa
- Spaghetti Squash
- Steamed Asparagus
- Scalloped Potatoes
- Balsamic Brussels Sprouts
- Garlic Butter Green Beans
- Maple Ginger Carrots
- Garlic Herb Mashed Potatoes
- Parmesan Zucchini Noodles
- Black Eyed Peas
- Tomato White Beans
- Curried Lentils

Cilantro Lime Rice

Yield: makes 8 servings

Prep Time: 5 minutes

Cook Time: 12 minutes

In the Pot Time: 25 minutes

Total Time: 30 minutes

Function Buttons: Rice

Ingredients:

- 1 ½ cups vegetable broth
- ¾ cup water
- 2 tablespoons olive oil
- 3 tablespoons fresh lime juice, divided
- 2 cups long-grain white rice, uncooked
- 1/2 bunch fresh cilantro, chopped
- Salt to taste

Instructions:

1. Combine the vegetable broth, water, and olive oil in the Instant Pot.
2. Stir in the rice and 2 tablespoons lime juice.
3. Close and lock the lid then press the Rice button – it should automatically cook for about 12 minutes.
4. When the timer goes off, allow the steam to vent naturally for 5 minutes then switch the steam release valve to the "venting" position to Quick Release the remaining steam.

5. When the float valve drops down, unlock and open the lid.
6. Spoon the rice into a large serving bowl and toss with the remaining lime juice as well as the cilantro and salt.

Nutrition: 205 calories per serving, 4.1g fat, 4.2g protein, 37.2g carbs. 0.6g fiber

Wild Rice

Yield: makes 8 servings

Prep Time: none

Cook Time: 35 minutes

In the Pot Time: 45 minutes

Total Time: 45 minutes

Function Buttons: Manual

Ingredients:

- 3 cups water
- 2 cups vegetable broth
- 2 cups wild rice, uncooked

Instructions:

1. Combine the water, broth, rice, and salt in the Instant Pot.
2. Close and lock the lid then press the Manual button and adjust the timer to 35 minutes.
3. When the timer goes off, press the Cancel button and switch the steam release valve to the "venting" position to Quick Release the steam.
4. When the float valve drops down, unlock and open the lid.
5. Fluff the rice with a fork then spoon into a bowl to serve.

Nutrition: 150 calories per serving, 0.8g fat, 7.1g protein, 30.1g carbs, 2.5g fiber

Basic Quinoa

Yield: makes 8 servings

Prep Time: 5 minutes

Cook Time: 1 minute

In the Pot Time: 25 minutes

Total Time: 30 minutes

Function Buttons: Manual

Ingredients:

- 2 cups uncooked quinoa
- 1 cups vegetable broth
- Salt to taste

Instructions:

1. Rinse the quinoa thoroughly in cool water then add it to the Instant Pot.
2. Add the broth and salt then close and lock the lid.
3. Press the Manual button and adjust the timer to 1 minute.
4. When the timer goes off, allow the steam to vent naturally for 15 minutes then switch the steam release valve to the "venting" position to Quick Release any remaining steam.
5. When the float valve drops down, unlock and open the lid.
6. Fluff the quinoa with a fork then spoon into a bowl to serve.

Nutrition: 160 calories per serving, 2.8g fat, 6.6g protein, 27.4g carbs, 3g fiber

Spaghetti Squash

Yield: makes 6 servings

Prep Time: 5 minutes

Cook Time: 5 minutes

In the Pot Time: 25 minutes

Total Time: 30 minutes

Function Buttons: Manual

Ingredients:

- 1 medium spaghetti squash (about 4 pounds)
- 1 cup water
- 2 tablespoons butter
- Salt and pepper

Instructions:

1. Cut the spaghetti squash in half then scoop out the seeds.
2. Place the squash halves in the Instant Pot cut-sides up then pour in the water.
3. Close and lock the lid then press the Manual button and adjust the timer to 5 minutes.
4. When the timer goes off, press the Cancel button and switch the steam release valve to the "venting" position to Quick Release the steam.
5. When the float valve drops down, unlock and open the lid.
6. Remove the squash halves and shred the flesh with two forks into a bowl.
7. Add the butter then season with salt and pepper and serve hot.

Nutrition: 70 calories per serving, 4.3g fat, 0.9g protein, 8.3g carbs, 1.8g fiber

Steamed Asparagus

Yield: makes 4 servings

Prep Time: none

Cook Time: 2 minutes

In the Pot Time: 15 minutes

Total Time: 15 minutes

Function Buttons: Steam

Ingredients:

- 1 pound asparagus
- 1 cup water
- 1 tablespoon butter
- Salt and pepper

Instructions:

1. Place the steamer insert in the Instant Pot and pour in 1 cup water.
2. Arrange the asparagus spears on the steamer insert.
3. Close and lock the lid then press the Steam button and adjust the timer to 2 minutes.
4. When the timer goes off, press the Cancel button and switch the steam release valve to the "venting" position to Quick Release the steam.
5. When the float valve drops down, unlock and open the lid.
6. Lift the steamer basket out of the Instant Pot and transfer the asparagus to a serving bowl.
7. Top with butter and season with salt and pepper to taste.

Nutrition: 50 calories per serving, 3g fat, 2.5g protein, 4.4g carbs, 2.4g fiber

Scalloped Potatoes

Yield: makes 6 servings

Prep Time: 15 minutes (including broiling time)

Cook Time: 1 minute

In the Pot Time: 15 minutes

Total Time: 30 minutes

Function Buttons: Manual, Sauté

Ingredients:

- 2 pounds small potatoes, washed
- 1 cup vegetable broth
- ¼ cup heavy cream
- 2 cups shredded cheese (try white cheddar)
- ¾ teaspoon garlic powder
- ½ teaspoon dried thyme
- Salt and pepper

Instructions:

1. Slice the potatoes into ¼-inch slices and place them in the Instant Pot.
2. Add the vegetable broth then close and lock the lid.
3. Press the Manual button and adjust the timer to 1 minute.
4. When the timer goes off, press the Cancel button and switch the steam release valve to the "venting" position to Quick Release the steam.
5. When the float valve drops down, unlock and open the lid.
6. Spoon the potatoes into an oven-safe dish then set aside.

7. Pour the heavy cream into the Instant Pot then add 1 ½ cups shredded cheese along with the garlic powder, thyme, salt and pepper.
8. Press the Sauté button and cook, stirring often, until the cheese is melted into a smooth sauce.
9. Pour the sauce over the potatoes then top with the remaining cheese.
10. Broil for 4 to 6 minutes until the cheese is melted and browned then serve hot.

Nutrition: 280 calories per serving, 14.7g fat, 12.9g protein, 24.8g carbs, 3.7g fiber

Balsamic Brussels Sprouts

Yield: makes 4 servings

Prep Time: 5 minutes

Cook Time: 2 minutes

In the Pot Time: 20 minutes

Total Time: 25 minutes

Function Buttons: Manual, Sauté

Ingredients:

- 1 pound fresh brussels sprouts, trimmed and cut in half
- 4 slices bacon, chopped
- 2 cups water
- 3 tablespoons balsamic vinegar
- Salt and pepper

Instructions:

1. Place the steamer basket in the Instant Pot and pour in 2 cups water.
2. Place the brussels sprouts in the steamer insert.
3. Close and lock the lid then press the Manual button and adjust the timer to 2 minutes.
4. When the timer goes off, press the Cancel button and switch the steam release valve to the "venting" position to Quick Release the steam.
5. When the float valve drops down, unlock and open the lid.
6. Transfer the steamed brussels sprouts to a bowl then remove the insert from the Instant Pot and empty the water.
7. Press the Sauté button and add the bacon to the Instant Pot.
8. Cook for 2 minutes then add the brussels sprouts and balsamic vinegar, stirring well, and cook for another 5 minutes until browned and fragrant
9. Season the brussels sprouts with salt and pepper to serve.

Nutrition: 50 calories per serving, 0.4g fat, 3.9g protein, 10.4g carbs, 4.3g fiber

Garlic Butter Green Beans

Yield: makes 4 servings

Prep Time: 5 minutes

Cook Time: 5 minutes

In the Pot Time: 15 minutes

Total Time: 20 minutes

Function Buttons: Manual

Ingredients:

- 1 pound fresh green beans, ends trimmed
- 1 ¼ cups water
- 2 tablespoons butter
- 2 cloves minced garlic
- Salt and pepper

Instructions:

1. Place the green beans in the Instant Pot.
2. Add the water, butter, and garlic then toss to coat and season with salt and pepper.
3. Close and lock the lid then press the Manual button and set the timer to 5 minutes.
4. When the timer goes off, press the Cancel button and switch the steam release valve to the "venting" position to Quick Release the steam.
5. When the float valve drops down, unlock and open the lid.
6. Spoon the beans into a serving bowl and serve hot.

Nutrition: 90 calories per serving, 5.9g fat, 2.2g protein, 8.6g carbs, 3.9g fiber

Maple Ginger Carrots

Yield: makes 4 servings

Prep Time: 5 minutes

Cook Time: 2 minutes

In the Pot Time: 15 minutes

Total Time: 20 minutes

Function Buttons: Manual

Ingredients:

- 8 large carrots, sliced ¼-inch thick
- 3 tablespoons maple syrup
- 1 teaspoon ground ginger
- 1 teaspoon salt
- 1/3 cup water

Instructions:

1. Toss the carrots with the maple syrup, ground ginger, and salt in the Instant Pot.
2. Pour in the water and stir well.
3. Close and lock the lid then press the Manual button and adjust the timer to 2 minutes.
4. When the timer goes off, press the Cancel button and switch the steam release valve to the "venting" position to Quick Release the steam.
5. When the float valve drops down, unlock and open the lid.
6. Spoon the carrots into a bowl and serve hot.

Nutrition: 100 calories per serving, 0.1g fat, 1.2g protein, 24.5g carbs, 3.6g fiber

Garlic Herb Mashed Potatoes

Yield: makes 6 servings

Prep Time: 10 minutes

Cook Time: 8 minutes

In the Pot Time: 20 minutes

Total Time: 30 minutes

Function Buttons: Manual

Ingredients:

- 2 ½ pounds russet potatoes, peeled and quartered
- 3 cups water
- 1 ½ tablespoons minced garlic
- 1 teaspoon fresh chopped rosemary
- 1 teaspoon fresh chopped chives
- Salt and pepper
- ¼ cup butter softened
- ¼ cup sour cream
- 4 ounces cream cheese, softened
- 2 tablespoons fresh chopped chives

Instructions:

1. Place the potatoes in the Instant Pot then add the water, garlic, rosemary, and thyme – season with salt and pepper.
2. Close and lock the lid then press the Manual button and adjust the timer to 8 minutes.
3. When the timer goes off, press the Cancel button and switch the steam release valve to the "venting" position to Quick Release the steam.
4. When the float valve drops down, unlock and open the lid.
5. Mash the potatoes with a potato masher then stir in the butter, sour cream, cream cheese, and chives.
6. Adjust seasoning to taste then spoon into a large bowl to serve.

Nutrition: 290 calories per serving, 16.5g fat, 5.2g protein, 31.5g carbs, 4.7g fiber

Parmesan Zucchini Noodles

Yield: makes 4 servings

Prep Time: 5 minutes

Cook Time: 3 minutes

In the Pot Time: 5 minutes

Total Time: 5 minutes

Function Buttons: Sauté

Ingredients:

- 3 tablespoons olive oil
- 1 tablespoon fresh lemon zest
- 3 cloves minced garlic
- ½ teaspoon salt
- 3 large zucchini, spiralized
- 2 tablespoons fresh lemon juice
- 1/3 cup grated parmesan cheese
- Salt and pepper

Instructions:

1. Press the Sauté button on the Instant Pot and wait for the display to read "hot."
2. Add the olive oil, lemon zest, garlic, and salt and cook for 30 seconds, stirring.
3. Add the zucchini noodles and lemon juice, tossing to coat.
4. Cook for 1 to 2 minutes until just tender then sprinkle with parmesan.
5. Stir the cheese through the noodles then season with salt and pepper to serve.

Nutrition: 175 calories per serving, 13.3g fat, 6.2g protein, 9.4g carbs, 2.8g fiber

Black Eyed Peas

Yield: makes 6 servings

Prep Time: 15 minutes

Cook Time: 15 minutes

In the Pot Time: 45 minutes

Total Time: 1 hour

Function Buttons: Sauté, Manual

Ingredients:

- 1 tablespoon olive oil
- 1 medium yellow onion, chopped
- 1 small red pepper, chopped
- 2 small celery stalks, chopped
- 2 small bay leaves
- 1 ½ tablespoons smoked paprika
- ½ teaspoon dried thyme
- Salt and pepper
- 3 cloves minced garlic
- 3 ½ cups vegetable broth
- 1 tablespoon balsamic vinegar
- 2 slices bacon, chopped
- 1 small ham hock
- 1 ¼ cup dry black-eyed peas
- 2 cups fresh chopped collard greens

Instructions:

1. Press the Sauté button and wait for the display panel on the Instant Pot to read "hot."
2. Add the oil then stir in the onion, celery, and peppers.
3. Stir in the bay leaf then cook for 2 to 3 minutes until the onions are translucent.
4. Add the paprika and thyme then season with salt and pepper.
5. Stir in the garlic then cook for 30 seconds more, stirring often.
6. Add the chicken broth, balsamic vinegar, and bacon then add the ham hock.
7. Stir in the black-eyed peas and collard greens.
8. Press the Cancel button then close and lock the lid.
9. Press the Manual button and adjust the timer to 15 minutes.
10. When the timer goes off, allow the steam to vent naturally for 15 minutes then switch the steam release valve to the "venting" position to Quick Release the remaining steam.
11. When the float valve drops down, unlock and open the lid.
12. Discard the bay leaves and ham hock then stir well.
13. Adjust seasoning to taste and spoon into a large bowl to serve.

Nutrition: 290 calories per serving, 9.6g fat, 22.9g protein, 39g carbs, 14.9g fiber

Tomato White Beans

Yield: makes 6 servings

Prep Time: 10 minutes

Cook Time: 35 minutes

In the Pot Time: 1 hour

Total Time: 1 hour 10 minutes

Function Buttons: Sauté, Manual

Ingredients:

- 4 slices bacon, chopped
- 1 medium yellow onion, chopped
- 3 cloves minced garlic
- 2 (14-ounce) cans whole peeled tomatoes
- 2 cups dry white cannellini beans
- 2 cups chicken broth
- 1 (6-ounce) can tomato paste
- 1 small bay leaf
- Salt and pepper

Instructions:

1. Press the Sauté button on the Instant Pot and wait for the display to read "hot."
2. Add the bacon and cook until the fat renders and the bacon starts to crisp up.
3. Stir in the onions and garlic then cook for 3 minutes until the onions are translucent.
4. Add the tomatoes, beans, chicken broth, tomato paste, and bay leaf.
5. Stir well then close and lock the lid.
6. Press the Manual button and adjust the timer to 35 minutes.

7. When the timer goes off, allow the steam to vent naturally and, when the float valve drops down, unlock and open the lid.
8. Discard the bay leaf then stir everything well and season with salt and pepper to taste.

Nutrition: 175 calories per serving, 3.5g fat, 11.4g protein, 27.1g carbs, 5.9g fiber

Curried Lentils

Yield: makes 8 servings

Prep Time: 10 minutes

Cook Time: 5 minutes

In the Pot Time: 25 minutes

Total Time: 35 minutes

Function Buttons: Sauté, Manual

Ingredients:

- 2 cups dried lentils
- 2 tablespoons olive oil
- 1 medium yellow onion, chopped
- 1 large stalk celery, diced
- 1 large carrot, peeled and diced
- ½ tablespoon curry powder
- 1 1/2 cups vegetable broth
- 1 (14-ounce) can coconut milk
- 1 medium tomato, diced
- 2 tablespoons fresh lime juice
- Salt and pepper

Instructions:

1. Rinse the lentils well then set them aside.
2. Press the Sauté button on the Instant Pot and wait for the display to read "hot."
3. Add the oil then stir in the onions, celery, and carrot – cook for 5 minutes, stirring occasionally.
4. Stir in the curry powder along with the lentils, vegetable broth, coconut milk, and tomatoes.
5. Close and lock the lid then press the Manual button and adjust the timer to 5 minutes.
6. When the timer goes off, allow the steam to vent naturally for 10 minutes then switch the steam release valve to the "venting" position to Quick Release the remaining steam.
7. When the float valve drops down, unlock and open the lid.
8. Stir in the lime juice then adjust seasoning to taste. Spoon into a bowl to serve.

Nutrition: 335 calories per serving, 16.2g fat, 14.8g protein, 35g carbs, 16.7g fiber

Seafood Recipes

Recipes Included in this Chapter:

- Chili Lime Shrimp Pasta
- Simple Seafood Gumbo
- Shrimp Paella
- Salmon with Ginger Citrus Sauce
- Buttery Shrimp Scampi
- Spicy Coconut Fish Curry
- Lemon Pepper Salmon
- Garlic Steamed Mussels
- Quick and Easy Fish Tacos
- Easy Steamed Clams
- Spicy Pineapple Shrimp and Rice
- Chili Lime Salmon Fillets

Chili Lime Shrimp Pasta

Yield: makes 6 servings

Prep Time: 5 minutes

Cook Time: 4 minutes

In the Pot Time: 30 minutes

Total Time: 35 minutes

Function Buttons: Manual, Sauté

Ingredients:

- 1 pound spaghetti pasta, uncooked
- 4 ¼ cups water
- 1 teaspoon coconut oil, melted
- 1 tablespoon minced garlic
- 1 teaspoon salt
- ¾ cup mayonnaise
- ¾ cup sweet chili sauce
- 2 limes, juiced
- 1 tablespoon sriracha sauce
- 1 pound large shrimp, peeled and deveined
- 4 scallions, sliced thin

Instructions:

1. Break the spaghetti noodles in half and place them in the Instant Pot.
2. Add the water, coconut oil, garlic, and salt then close and lock the lid.
3. Press the Manual button and adjust the timer to 4 minutes.

4. When the timer goes off, press the Cancel button and switch the steam release valve to the "venting" position to Quick Release the steam.
5. Wait for the float valve to drop back down then unlock and open the lid.
6. While the pasta is cooking, whisk together the mayonnaise, sweet chili sauce, lime juice, and sriracha together in a bowl.
7. Pour the sauce over the cooked pasta then add the shrimp and scallions – stir well to combine.
8. Press the Sauté button and cook for 2 to 3 minutes, stirring often, until the shrimp are just cooked through.
9. Season with salt and pepper to taste then serve hot.

Nutrition: 600 calories per serving, 21.9g fat, 24.4g protein, 72.4g carbs, 2.8g fiber

Simple Seafood Gumbo

Yield: makes 8 servings

Prep Time: 10 minutes

Cook Time: 5 minutes

In the Pot Time: 35 minutes

Total Time: 45 minutes

Function Buttons: Sauté, Manual, Keep Warm

Ingredients:

- 24 ounces boneless white fish fillets
- Salt and pepper
- 3 tablespoons butter
- 2 tablespoons Cajun seasoning (plus extra)
- 2 medium yellow onions, chopped
- 2 medium red peppers, chopped
- 3 large stalks celery, diced
- 2 (14-ounce) cans diced tomatoes
- ¼ cup tomato paste
- 1 ½ cups chicken broth
- 2 large bay leaves
- 2 pounds large shrimp, peeled and deveined

Instructions:

1. Season the fish with salt and pepper and sprinkle with Cajun seasoning, coating the fish as evenly as possible.
2. Press the Sauté button on the Instant Pot and add the butter – wait for the display panel to read "hot."
3. Add the fish to the Instant Pot and cook for 2 minutes then turn and cook for 2 minutes on the other side – it should be browned on both sides.
4. Remove the fish to a plate and add the onions, peppers, and celery to the Instant Pot.
5. Add some more Cajun seasoning then sauté for 2 minutes.
6. Press the Keep Warm button then add the cooked fish along with the tomatoes, tomato paste, broth, and bay leaves to the Instant Pot.
7. Stir everything well then close and lock the lid.

8. Press the Manual button and set the timer for 5 minutes.
9. When the timer goes off, press the Cancel button and switch the steam release valve to the "venting" position to Quick Release the pressure.
10. Wait for the float valve to drop back down then unlock and open the lid.
11. Stir in the shrimp then press the Sauté button and cook for 3 to 4 minutes until just opaque.
12. Season with salt and pepper to taste then serve hot over steamed rice.

Nutrition: 255 calories per serving, 5.2g fat, 41.3g protein, 13.3g carbs, 2.9g fiber

Shrimp Paella

Yield: makes 4 servings

Prep Time: 5 minutes

Cook Time: 5 minutes

In the Pot Time: 30 minutes

Total Time: 35 minutes

Function Buttons: Sauté, Manual

Ingredients:

- ¼ cup butter
- 1 medium yellow onion, chopped
- 3 cloves minced garlic
- 1 ¼ teaspoon ground turmeric
- ¾ teaspoon paprika
- Salt and pepper
- ¼ teaspoon red pepper flakes
- 1 cup uncooked Arborio rice
- 2 1/2 cups Chicken Broth
- 1 pound uncooked shrimp, peeled and deveined
- Fresh chopped cilantro

Instructions:

1. Press the Sauté button on the Instant Pot then add the butter and wait for the display panel to read "hot."
2. Add the onions and cook for 2 minutes until softened then stir in the garlic and cook for 1 minute more.
3. Stir in the turmeric, paprika, salt, pepper, and red pepper flakes (if using) then cook for 1 minute.
4. Add the rice and stir well then cook for 1 minute before adding the chicken broth and white wine.
5. Place the shrimp on top of the rice then close and lock the lid.
6. Press the Manual button and set the timer to 5 minutes.
7. When the timer goes off, press the Cancel button and switch the steam release valve to the "venting" position to Quick Release the steam.
8. When the float valve drops down, unlock and open the lid.
9. Spoon the paella into bowls and serve garnished with fresh cilantro.

Nutrition: 415 calories per serving, 13.6g fat, 29.5g protein, 41.8g carbs, 3g fiber

Salmon with Ginger Citrus Sauce

Yield: makes 4 servings

Prep Time: 5 minutes (plus 30 minutes marinade time)

Cook Time: 3 minutes

In the Pot Time: 20 minutes

Total Time: 25 minutes

Function Buttons: Manual

Ingredients:

- 2 tablespoons orange marmalade
- 1 ½ tablespoons soy sauce
- 2 teaspoons fresh grated ginger
- 2 cloves minced garlic
- 4 (4-ounce) boneless salmon fillets
- Salt and pepper

Instructions:

1. Whisk together the orange marmalade, soy sauce, ginger, and garlic in a small bowl.
2. Season the salmon fillets with salt and pepper then place them in a zippered freezer bag.
3. Pour in the sauce then shake to coat and marinate for 30 minutes.
4. Place the steamer rack in the Instant Pot and pour in 2 cups of water.
5. Put the freezer bag in the steamer rack then close and lock the lid.
6. Press the Manual button and set the timer to 3 minutes.
7. When the timer goes off, allow the pressure to vent naturally for 5 minutes then press the Cancel button and switch the steam release valve to the "venting" position.
8. When the float valve drops down, unlock and open the lid.
9. Transfer the fillets to a greased baking sheet and broil for 3 to 4 minutes until browned. Serve hot.

Nutrition: 185 calories per serving, 7.1g fat, 22.6g protein, 8.3g carbs, 0.3g fiber

Buttery Shrimp Scampi

Yield: makes 6 servings

Prep Time: 5 minutes

Cook Time: 1 minute

In the Pot Time: 15 minutes

Total Time: 20 minutes

Function Buttons: Sauté, Meat/Stew

Ingredients:

- 2 tablespoons olive oil
- 2 tablespoons butter
- 3 cloves minced garlic
- ½ cup white wine
- ½ cup chicken broth
- 2 pounds large shrimp, peeled and deveined
- 3 cups steamed white rice
- 1 tablespoon fresh lemon juice
- Salt and pepper
- Fresh chopped parsley

Instructions:

1. Press the Sauté button on the Instant Pot then wait for the display panel to read "hot."
2. Add the oil and butter then stir in the garlic and cook for 1 minute.
3. Pour in the white wine and chicken broth, scraping up any browned bits from the bottom of the pot.
4. Press the Cancel button then add the shrimp and close and lock the lid.
5. Press the Meat/Stew button and adjust the timer to 1 minute.
6. When the timer goes off, allow the pressure to vent naturally for 5 minutes then press the Cancel Button.
7. Switch the steam release to the "venting" position to vent the remaining steam.
8. When the float valve drops down, unlock and open the lid.
9. Stir in the rice and lemon juice then season with salt and pepper.
10. Serve hot garnished with fresh parsley.

Nutrition: 555 calories per serving, 9.3g fat, 35.2g protein, 77.8g carbs, 1.2g fiber

Spicy Coconut Fish Curry

Yield: makes 6 servings

Prep Time: 10 minutes

Cook Time: 5 minutes

In the Pot Time: 25 minutes

Total Time: 35 minutes

Function Buttons: Sauté, Manual

Ingredients:

- 1 teaspoon coconut oil
- 6 medium curry leaves
- 2 medium yellow onions, sliced
- 1 tablespoon fresh grated ginger
- 3 cloves minced garlic
- 1 tablespoon ground coriander
- ½ tablespoon ground cumin
- 1 teaspoon chili powder

- ½ teaspoon ground turmeric
- 2 cups unsweetened coconut milk (not canned)
- 2 small green chiles, sliced
- 1 medium tomato, diced
- 1 ½ pounds white fish fillets, cut into bite-sized pieces
- Salt and pepper
- 1 tablespoon fresh lemon juice
- Steamed rice, to serve

Instructions:

1. Press the Sauté button then add the oil and wait for the Instant Pot display panel to read "hot."
2. Add the curry leaves and fry for 1 minute until golden brown then stir in the onion, ginger, and garlic.
3. Cook for 3 minutes until the onion is tender then stir in the ground spices and cook for 2 minutes, stirring occasionally.
4. Pour in the coconut milk and scrape up any browned bits from the bottom of the pot.
5. Stir in the green chiles, tomatoes, and fish until the fish is coated then close and lock the lid.
6. Press the Manual button and set the timer for 5 minutes.
7. When the timer goes off, press the Cancel button and switch the steam release valve to the "venting" position to Quick Release the steam.
8. When the float valve drops down, unlock and open the lid.
9. Season with salt and pepper then stir in the lemon juice and serve hot over steamed rice.

Nutrition: 265 calories per serving, 11.3g fat, 29g protein, 10g carbs, 1.1g fiber

Lemon Pepper Salmon

Yield: makes 4 servings

Prep Time: 10 minutes

Cook Time: 5 minutes

In the Pot Time: 20 minutes

Total Time: 30 minutes

Function Buttons: Steam, Sauté

Ingredients:

- ¾ cup water
- 4 sprigs fresh parsley
- 1 sprig fresh tarragon
- 1 large leaf basil
- 1 tablespoon olive oil
- Salt and pepper
- 1 pound boneless salmon fillet, skin-on
- ½ large lemon, sliced thin
- 1 large carrot, sliced
- 1 medium zucchini, sliced
- 1 red pepper, sliced thin
- 1 green pepper, sliced thin

Instructions:

1. Pour the water into the Instant Pot then add the parsley, tarragon, and basil.
2. Place the steamer insert in the Instant Pot then place the salmon on top of it, skin-side down.
3. Brush the salmon with oil then season with salt and pepper – place the lemon slices on top of the salmon.
4. Close and lock the lid then press the Steam button and adjust the time to 3 minutes.
5. When the timer goes off, press the Cancel button and switch the steam release valve to the "venting" position to Quick Release the steam.
6. When the float valve drops down, unlock and open the lid.
7. Remove the salmon to a serving plate then scoop out and discard the herbs.
8. Add the veggies to the Instant Pot then close the lid and press the Sauté button.
9. Let the veggies cook for 1 to 2 minutes until tender then spoon into a bowl and serve with the salmon.

Nutrition: 215 calories per serving, 10.7g fat, 23.4g protein, 7.1g carbs, 1.9g fiber

Garlic Steamed Mussels

Yield: makes 4 servings

Prep Time: 5 minutes

Cook Time: 5 minutes

In the Pot Time: 25 minutes

Total Time: 30 minutes

Function Buttons: Sauté, Manual

Ingredients:

- 2 tablespoons butter
- 2 pounds live mussels
- 1 small yellow onion, diced
- 3 cloves minced garlic
- ½ cup chicken broth
- ½ cup white wine
- 2 tablespoons fresh chopped parsley

Instructions:

1. Clean the mussels in cool water, removing the beards and discarding any that do not close (they are already dead).
2. Combine the butter and onions in the Instant Pot and press the Sauté button.
3. Cook the onions for 3 minutes until translucent, stirring often, then add the garlic.
4. Let the garlic cook for 1 minute then pour in the broth and wine, scraping up any browned bits on the bottom of the pot.
5. Press the Cancel button then add the mussels.
6. Close and lock the lid then press the Manual button and adjust the time to 5 minutes.
7. When the timer goes off, allow the steam to vent naturally and, when the float valve drops down, unlock and open the lid.

8. Sprinkle the parsley over top of the mussels. Spoon the mussels into a serving bowl and serve with fresh lemon and melted butter.

Nutrition: 285 calories per serving, 11g fat, 28g protein, 11.7g carbs, 0.4g fiber

Quick and Easy Fish Tacos

Yield: makes 2 servings

Prep Time: 5 minutes

Cook Time: 8 minutes

In the Pot Time: 20 minutes

Total Time: 25 minutes

Function Buttons: Manual

Ingredients:

- 2 (6-ounce) boneless tilapia fillets
- 1 tablespoon olive oil
- Salt and pepper
- 2 slices lemon
- Pinch paprika

Instructions:

1. Cut two pieces of parchment paper and place a tilapia fillet in the middle of each.
2. Brush the fillets with oil then season with salt and pepper – place a lemon slice and a sprinkle of paprika on each fillet.
3. Fold the parchment paper into packets then place them on the steamer insert in your Instant Pot – pour in 1 ½ cups of water under the insert.
4. Close and lock the lid then press the Manual button and adjust the timer to 8 minutes.
5. When the timer goes off, press the Cancel button and switch the steam release valve to the "venting" position to Quick Release the steam.
6. When the float valve drops down, unlock and open the lid.
7. Remove the fish packets and chop the fillets into large pieces.
8. Serve the fish in warmed tortillas with your favorite taco toppings.

Nutrition: 250 calories per serving, 13.3g fat, 31.3g protein, 1.1g carbs, 1.1g fiber

Easy Steamed Clams

Yield: makes 4 servings

Prep Time: 5 minutes

Cook Time: 4 minutes

In the Pot Time: 20 minutes

Total Time: 25 minutes

Function Buttons: Sauté, Manual

Ingredients:

- 3 tablespoons olive oil
- 3 cloves minced garlic
- ¼ cup fresh chopped basil
- 2 cups beer (pale ale)
- ¾ cup water
- ¾ cup chicken broth
- ¼ cup white wine (dry)
- 2 tablespoons fresh lemon juice
- 3 pounds fresh clams, cleaned well

Instructions:

1. Pour the oil into the Instant Pot and press the Sauté button then wait for the display panel to read "hot."
2. Add the garlic and cook for 1 minute then stir in the basil and cook 30 seconds more.
3. Stir in beer, water, chicken broth, and wine then add the lemon juice and cook for 1 minute until hot.
4. Place the steamer insert in the Instant Pot then place the clams in the basket.
5. Close and lock the lid then press the Manual button and adjust the timer to 4 minutes.
6. When the timer goes off, press the Cancel button and switch the steam release valve to the "venting" position to Quick Release the steam.
7. When the float valve drops down, unlock and open the lid.
8. Discard any clams that haven't opened then serve the rest hot with the cooking liquid spooned over top.

Nutrition: 205 calories per serving, 11.3g fat, 8.2g protein, 7g carbs, 0.1g fiber

Spicy Pineapple Shrimp and Rice

Yield: makes 6 servings

Prep Time: 5 minutes

Cook Time: 2 minutes

In the Pot Time: 20 minutes

Total Time: 25 minutes

Function Buttons: Manual

Ingredients:

- 12 ounces short-grain white rice, uncooked
- 1 large red bell pepper, chopped
- ½ cup unsweetened pineapple juice
- ¼ cup white wine (dry)
- 2 ½ tablespoons soy sauce
- 1 ½ tablespoons sweet chili sauce
- 1 tablespoon chili paste
- 1 pound large shrimp, peeled and deveined
- 1 ½ cups canned pineapple chunks

- 3 green onions, sliced thin

Instructions:

1. Combine the rice, bell peppers, pineapple juice, wine, soy sauce, chili sauce, and chili paste in the Instant Pot.
2. Stir well then place the shrimp on top.
3. Close and lock the lid then press the Manual button and adjust the timer to 2 minutes.
4. When the timer goes off, allow the steam to vent naturally for 10 minutes then switch the steam release valve to the "venting" position to Quick Release the remaining steam.
5. When the float valve drops down, unlock and open the lid.
6. Stir in the pineapple and green onion and serve hot.

Nutrition: 330 calories per serving, 0.8g fat, 19.1g protein, 59.6g carbs, 2.7g fiber

Chili Lime Salmon Fillets

Yield: makes 4 servings

Prep Time: 5 minutes

Cook Time: 5 minutes

In the Pot Time: 20 minutes

Total Time: 25 minutes

Function Buttons: Steam

Ingredients:

- 1 cup water
- 4 (4-ounce) boneless salmon fillets
- Salt and pepper
- 2 limes, juiced
- 2 tablespoons olive oil
- 1 ½ tablespoons honey
- 1 tablespoon hot water
- 1 to 2 jalapenos, seeded and minced
- 3 cloves minced garlic
- 2 tablespoons fresh chopped parsley
- 1 teaspoon paprika
- ½ teaspoon ground cumin

Instructions:

1. Pour the water into the Instant Pot and place the steamer insert inside.
2. Place the salmon on top of the steamer rack then season with salt and pepper.
3. Close and lock the lid then press the Steam button and adjust the timer to 5 minutes.
4. Meanwhile, whisk together the lime juice, olive oil, honey, and water in a small bowl.
5. Whisk in the jalapeno, parsley, garlic, cumin, and paprika then set aside.
6. Switch the steam release valve to the "venting" position to Quick Release the steam when done.
7. When the float valve drops down, unlock and open the lid.
8. Transfer the salmon to a serving plate and drizzle with the sauce to serve.

Nutrition: 280 calories per serving, 15.9g fat, 27.9g protein, 8.9g carbs, 0.5g fiber

Beef and Lamb Recipes

Recipes Included in this Chapter:

- Beef Bourguignon
- Rosemary Leg of Lamb
- Shredded Roast Beef
- Greek-Style Roasted Lamb
- Braised Short Ribs
- Curried Lamb Stew with Chickpeas
- Meatloaf with Red Sauce
- Herbed Lamb Chops
- Korean-Style Beef
- Braised Lamb Shanks with Tomato Sauce
- Easy Bolognese Pasta
- Lamb and Vegetable Curry
- Hearty Beef Stroganoff
- Lamb and Sweet Potato Stew

Beef Bourguignon

Yield: makes 6 servings

Prep Time: 10 minutes

Cook Time: 30 minutes

In the Pot Time: 1 hour

Total Time: 1 hour 10 minutes

Function Buttons: Sauté, Manual

Ingredients:

- 2 tablespoons olive oil
- 1 pound beef stew meat, chopped
- Salt and pepper
- 8 ounces bacon, chopped
- 4 large carrots, peeled and sliced
- 1 large red onion, chopped
- 3 cloves minced garlic
- 2 large sweet potatoes, chopped
- 1 cup dry red wine
- ½ cup beef broth
- 1 tablespoon maple syrup (optional)
- 2 tablespoons fresh chopped parsley
- 1 teaspoon fresh chopped thyme

Instructions:

1. Press the Sauté button on the Instant Pot and wait for the display to read "hot."
2. Add the oil and let it heat up while you season the beef with salt and pepper.
3. Add the beef to the Instant Pot and cook until browned, stirring as needed.
4. Stir in the bacon, carrots, onions, and garlic then cook until the onions are browned about 3 to 4 minutes.
5. Add the sweet potatoes, wine, beef broth, maple syrup, parsley, and thyme.
6. Stir well and season with salt and pepper.
7. Close and lock the lid then press the Manual button and adjust the timer to 30 minutes.
8. When the timer goes off, allow the steam to vent naturally and, when the float valve drops down, unlock and open the lid.
9. Stir the ingredients together then adjust seasoning to taste and serve hot.

Nutrition: 550 calories per serving, 25.5g fat, 39.3g protein, 32.6g carbs, 4.9g fiber

Rosemary Leg of Lamb

Yield: makes 8 servings

Prep Time: 15 minutes

Cook Time: 30 minutes

In the Pot Time: 50 minutes

Total Time: 1 hour 1 minutes

Function Buttons: Sauté, Meat/Stew

Ingredients:

- 2 tablespoons olive oil
- 1 (4-pound) boneless leg of lamb
- Salt and pepper
- 1 tablespoon minced garlic
- 2 tablespoons fresh chopped rosemary
- 1 tablespoon fresh chopped thyme

Instructions:

1. Press the Sauté button on the Instant Pot and wait for the display to read "hot."
2. Add the oil to the pot and let it heat up while you season the lamb with salt and pepper.
3. Add the lamb to the pot and cook for 2 minutes on each side until browned all over, about 8 to 10 minutes.
4. Remove the lamb to a cutting board and spread the garlic, rosemary, and thyme over it, rubbing it into the skin.
5. Place the steamer rack in the Instant Pot and pour in 2 cups of water.
6. Place the lamb on the rack then close and lock the lid.
7. Press the Meat/Stew button and adjust the timer to 30 minutes.
8. When the timer goes off, allow the steam to vent naturally and, when the float valve drops down, unlock and open the lid.
9. Transfer the lamb to a roasting pan and broil for 2 minutes until browned.
10. Remove the lamb to a cutting board and let rest 10 minutes before slicing to serve.

Nutrition: 460 calories per serving, 20.3g fat, 63.8g protein, 1g carbs, 0.4g fiber

Shredded Roast Beef

Yield: makes 6 servings

Prep Time: 15 minutes

Cook Time: 75 minutes

In the Pot Time: 1 hour 30 minutes

Total Time: 1 hour 45 minutes

Function Buttons: Sauté, Manual

Ingredients:

- 2 tablespoons olive oil
- 1 (3.5-pound) beef rump roast
- Salt and pepper
- 1 ¼ cup beef broth
- 1 tablespoon dried Italian seasoning
- 8 ounces pepperoncini

Instructions:

1. Press the Sauté button on the Instant Pot and wait for the display to read "hot."
2. Add the oil and let it heat up while you season the beef with salt and pepper.
3. Place the beef in the Instant Pot and cook for 2 minutes on each side to brown, about 8 to 10 minutes total.
4. Whisk together the beef broth and Italian seasoning then pour into the Instant Pot and add the pepperoncini.
5. Close and lock the lid then press the Manual button and adjust the timer to 75 minutes.
6. When the timer goes off, allow the steam to vent naturally and, when the float valve drops down, unlock and open the lid.
7. Shred the beef with two forks and stir everything together well.
8. Serve the shredded beef on toasted sandwich buns with the cooking liquid for dipping.

Nutrition: 450 calories per serving, 19.7g fat, 60.7g protein, 3.1g carbs, 0g fiber

Greek-Style Roasted Lamb

Yield: makes 6 servings

Prep Time: 10 minutes

Cook Time: 40 minutes

In the Pot Time: 1 hour

Total Time: 1 hour 10 minutes

Function Buttons: Manual

Ingredients:

- 1 (2 ½-pound) lamb shoulder, boneless
- 4 cloves garlic, sliced
- 1 tablespoon fresh chopped rosemary
- 1 teaspoon fresh chopped thyme
- 1 teaspoon fresh chopped oregano
- Salt and pepper
- 1 cup water

Instructions:

1. If the lamb shoulder is rolled up, cut the string on the lamb shoulder and unroll it.
2. Spread the garlic and herbs over the lamb and season with salt and pepper before rolling it back up.
3. Add the water to the Instant Pot then place the lamb inside.
4. Close and lock the lid then press the Manual button and adjust the timer to 40 minutes.
5. When the timer goes off, allow the steam to vent naturally for 10 minutes then switch the steam release valve to the "venting" position to Quick Release the remaining steam.
6. When the float valve drops down, unlock and open the lid.
7. Remove the lamb to a roasting pan then unroll it.
8. Place the roasting pan in the oven at 430 and cook for 10 minutes until browned.
9. When the lamb is browned, cut it into chunks and serve as desired.

Nutrition: 365 calories per serving, 19.8g fat, 42.1g protein, 1.3g carbs, 0.5g fiber

Braised Short Ribs

Yield: makes 6 servings

Prep Time: 15 minutes

Cook Time: 35 minutes

In the Pot Time: 50 minutes

Total Time: 1 hour 5 minutes

Function Buttons: Sauté, Manual

Ingredients:

- 1 tablespoon olive oil
- 2 pounds beef short ribs
- Salt and pepper
- 1 medium yellow onion, chopped
- 2 cloves minced garlic
- ½ cup dry red wine
- 6 tablespoons ketchup
- 2 tablespoons soy sauce
- 1 tablespoon Worcestershire sauce
- 1 tablespoon brown sugar

Instructions:

1. Press the Sauté button on the Instant Pot and wait for the display to read "hot."
2. Add the oil and let it heat up while you season the ribs with salt and pepper.
3. Place the ribs in the pot and cook for 2 minutes on each side to sear, about 6 to 8 minutes total.
4. Remove the ribs to a bowl and add the onions to the pot – cook for 3 to 4 minutes until translucent.
5. Stir in the garlic and cook for 1 minute then add the remaining ingredients.
6. Close and lock the lid then press the Manual button and adjust the timer to 35 minutes.
7. When the timer goes off, allow the steam to vent naturally for 5 minutes then switch the steam release valve to the "venting" position to Quick Release the remaining steam.
8. When the float valve drops down, unlock and open the lid.
9. Remove the short ribs to a serving bowl or platter then serve hot.

Nutrition: 655 calories per serving, 57.1g fat, 22.2g protein, 8.7g carbs, 0.5g fiber

Curried Lamb Stew with Chickpeas

Yield: makes 4 servings

Prep Time: 15 minutes

Cook Time: 50 minutes

In the Pot Time: 1 hour 15 minutes

Total Time: 1 hour 30 minutes

Function Buttons: Sauté, Manual

Ingredients:

- 2 tablespoons olive oil
- 1 medium onion, chopped
- 5 cloves minced garlic
- 1 teaspoon dried coriander
- 1 teaspoon ground cumin
- 1 teaspoon ground cinnamon
- 1 teaspoon ground turmeric
- Salt and pepper
- 1 ½ pounds boneless lamb shoulder, chopped
- 1 (15-ounce) can chickpeas, rinsed and drained
- 1 ¼ cups chicken broth
- ¼ cup red wine vinegar
- 2 tablespoons tomato paste
- 2 tablespoons brown sugar
- ¼ cup dried apricots, chopped

Instructions:

1. Press the Sauté button on the Instant Pot and wait for the display to read "hot."
2. Add the oil then stir in the onions and cook for 3 to 4 minutes until translucent.
3. Stir in the garlic and spices then add the lamb and season with salt and pepper.
4. Sauté for 5 minutes, stirring often, then add the remaining ingredients.
5. Close and lock the lid then press the Manual button and adjust the timer to 50 minutes.
6. When the timer goes off, allow the steam to vent naturally and, when the float valve drops down, unlock and open the lid.
7. Stir everything well then serve hot over steamed rice or quinoa.

Nutrition: 565 calories per serving, 21.4g fat, 55.7g protein, 36g carbs, 6.3g fiber

Meatloaf with Red Sauce

Yield: makes 8 servings

Prep Time: 10 minutes

Cook Time: 35 minutes

In the Pot Time: 55 minutes

Total Time: 1 hour 5 minutes

Function Buttons: Manual

Ingredients:

- 2 pounds lean ground beef (90% lean)
- 1 ½ cups plain breadcrumbs
- 1 cup parmesan cheese
- 4 large eggs, whisked well
- 3 cloves minced garlic
- ½ teaspoon dried oregano
- ½ teaspoon dried thyme
- 2/3 cup ketchup
- 1 ½ tablespoons brown sugar
- 1 tablespoon dry mustard
- 1 tablespoon Worcestershire sauce
- 2 large potatoes, cut into chunks
- 4 medium carrots, peeled and sliced
- 1 cup beef broth

Instructions:

1. Combine the beef, breadcrumbs, parmesan cheese, and eggs in a mixing bowl.
2. Stir in the garlic, herbs, salt and pepper and mix well by hand.
3. Whisk together the ketchup, brown sugar, mustard, and Worcestershire sauce in a small bowl and set aside.
4. Place the potatoes and carrots in the Instant Pot then pour in the beef broth.
5. Place the steamer insert in the pot over the vegetables.
6. Shape the meat mixture into a loaf and place it on the steamer rack (line it with foil if needed).
7. Spread half the sauce mixture over the meatloaf then close and lock the lid.

8. Press the Manual button and adjust the timer to 35 minutes.
9. When the timer goes off, press the Cancel button and switch the steam release valve to the "venting" position to Quick Release the steam.
10. When the float valve drops down, unlock and open the lid.
11. Remove the meatloaf to a serving dish and the vegetables to a bowl.
12. Spread the remaining sauce over the meatloaf then broil for 5 minutes before serving.

Nutrition: 520 calories per serving, 20.2g fat, 42.3g protein, 40.7g carbs, 4.2g fiber

Herbed Lamb Chops

Yield: makes 4 servings

Prep Time: 10 minutes

Cook Time: 2 minutes

In the Pot Time: 25 minutes

Total Time: 35 minutes

Function Buttons: Sauté, Manual

Ingredients:

- 2 tablespoons olive oil
- 3 pounds bone-in lamb chops
- 1 tablespoon fresh chopped rosemary
- Salt and pepper
- 2 tablespoons tomato paste
- 1 small yellow onion, diced
- 1 cup beef broth

Instructions:

1. Press the Sauté button on the Instant Pot and wait for the display to read "hot."
2. Add the oil to the pot while you spread the rosemary, salt, and pepper on the lamb chops.
3. Add the lamb chops to the pot in batches, browning them for 1 minute on each side.
4. Remove the lamb chops to a bowl then add the tomato paste and onion to the pot – sauté for 1 to 2 minutes, stirring often.
5. Pour in the beef broth and scrape up any browned bits then add the lamb back to the pot.
6. Close and lock the lid then press the Manual button and adjust the timer to 2 minutes.
7. When the timer goes off, press the Cancel button and switch the steam release valve to the "venting" position to Quick Release the steam.
8. When the float valve drops down, unlock and open the lid.
9. Remove the lamb chops to a serving platter and serve immediately.

Nutrition: 535 calories per serving, 25.5g fat, 70.8g protein, 3.9gcarbs, 1.1g fiber

Korean-Style Beef

Yield: makes 6 servings

Prep Time: 10 minutes

Cook Time: 15 minutes

In the Pot Time: 35 minutes

Total Time: 45 minutes

Function Buttons: Manual, Sauté (More)

Ingredients:

- ½ cup beef broth
- 6 tablespoons soy sauce
- 6 tablespoons brown sugar
- 1 tablespoon minced garlic
- 1 tablespoon grated ginger
- 1 tablespoon rice wine vinegar
- 1 tablespoon sesame oil
- Sriracha, to taste
- 1 (3-pound) boneless beef chuck roast, chopped
- Salt and pepper
- 3 tablespoons cold water
- 3 tablespoons cornstarch

Instructions:

1. Whisk together the beef broth, soy sauce, brown sugar, garlic, ginger, vinegar, and sesame oil in a small bowl.
2. Add sriracha to taste, stirring until well combined.
3. Place the roast in the Instant Pot then season with salt and pepper and pour the broth mixture over it.
4. Close and lock the lid then press the Manual button and adjust the timer to 15 minutes.
5. When the timer goes off, press the Cancel button and switch the steam release valve to the "venting" position to Quick Release the steam.
6. When the float valve drops down, unlock and open the lid.
7. Whisk together the water and cornstarch in a small bowl then stir it into the Instant Pot.
8. Press the Sauté button and adjust it to More – cook for 2 to 3 minutes until the sauce has thickened.
9. Serve hot garnished with sesame seeds and sliced green onion.

Nutrition: 575 calories per serving, 21.3g fat, 76.5g protein, 14.9g carbs, 0.3g fiber

Braised Lamb Shanks with Tomato Sauce

Yield: makes 4 servings

Prep Time: 15 minutes

Cook Time: 45 minutes

In the Pot Time: 1 hour 30 minutes

Total Time: 1 hour 45 minutes

Function Buttons: Sauté (More), Manual

Ingredients:

- 2 tablespoons olive oil
- 4 (1-pound) bone-in lamb shanks
- Salt and pepper
- 5 cloves minced garlic
- ¾ cup dry red wine
- 2 (14-ounce) cans crushed tomatoes
- 1 teaspoon dried basil
- ½ teaspoon dried oregano
- ½ teaspoon dried thyme

Instructions:

1. Press the Sauté button on the Instant Pot and adjust it to More then wait for the display to read "hot."
2. Add the oil to the pot and season the lamb with salt and pepper while waiting for it to heat up.
3. Place the lamb in the pot and cook until browned, about 4 minutes per side, then remove to a plate.
4. Add the garlic to the pot and cook for 30 seconds then pour in the wine, scraping up the browned bits from the bottom of the pot.
5. Stir in the tomatoes, basil, oregano, and thyme then cook for 2 minutes, stirring occasionally.
6. Place the lamb back in the pot then close and lock the lid.
7. Press the Manual button and adjust the timer to 45 minutes.
8. When the timer goes off, allow the steam to vent naturally for 15 minutes then switch the steam release valve to the "venting" position to Quick Release the remaining steam.
9. When the float valve drops down, unlock and open the lid.
10. Serve the lamb hot with the tomato sauce over cooked rice or pasta.

Nutrition: 605 calories per serving, 33.1g fat, 49.1g protein, 18.6g carbs, 6.6g fiber

Easy Bolognese Pasta

Yield: makes 6 servings

Prep Time: 45 minutes (including simmer)

Cook Time: 20 minutes

In the Pot Time: 1 hour 20 minutes

Total Time: 1 hour 45 minutes

Function Buttons: Sauté, Manual

Ingredients:

- 1 tablespoon olive oil
- 1 large yellow onion, chopped
- 2 medium carrots, peeled and chopped
- 2 stalks celery, chopped
- 1 pound lean ground beef (90% lean)
- ½ pound ground pork
- ¼ pound chopped bacon
- Salt and pepper
- 2 tablespoons tomato paste
- 1 teaspoon minced garlic
- ½ cup dry red wine
- 2 (14-ounce) cans crushed tomatoes
- ½ cup water
- ¼ cup fresh chopped parsley
- 1/4 cup heavy cream

Instructions:

1. Press the Sauté button on the Instant Pot and wait for the display to read "hot."
2. Add the oil and let it heat up then stir in the onions, carrots, and celery until browned – about 8 to 10 minutes.
3. Place the ground beef, ground pork, and bacon in the pot and season with salt and pepper.
4. Sauté the meat until browned, breaking it up with a spoon, about 10 to 15 minutes.
5. Stir in the tomato paste and garlic then cook for 1 minute.
6. Pour in the red wine and scrape up any browned bits at the bottom of the pot – simmer for 2 to 3 minutes until most of the wine cooks off.
7. Stir in the tomatoes, water, and parsley then bring to a simmer.
8. Close and lock the lid then press the Manual button and adjust the timer to 20 minutes.
9. When the timer goes off, press the Cancel button and switch the steam release valve to the "venting" position to Quick Release the steam.
10. When the float valve drops down, unlock and open the lid.
11. Press the Sauté button and let the sauce simmer, stirring often, for 10 minutes until thickened.
12. Stir in the cream then season with salt and pepper to taste. Serve hot over pasta.

Nutrition: 475 calories per serving, 26.3g fat, 37.4g protein, 17.4g carbs, 5.7g fiber

Lamb and Vegetable Curry

Yield: makes 6 servings

Prep Time: 35 minutes (including marinating)

Cook Time: 25 minutes

In the Pot Time: 1 hour

Total Time: 1 hour 35 minutes

Function Buttons: Sauté, Manual

Ingredients:

- 1 ½ pounds boneless lamb, chopped
- 1 tablespoon minced garlic
- 1 tablespoon fresh grated ginger
- ½ cup canned coconut milk
- 1 to 2 tablespoons fresh lime juice
- Salt and pepper
- 1 (14-ounce) can diced tomatoes
- 1 medium yellow onion, chopped
- 4 small carrots, peeled and sliced
- 1 tablespoon butter
- 1 ½ tablespoons curry powder
- 1 large zucchini, diced
- Fresh chopped cilantro

Instructions:

1. Combine the lamb, garlic, ginger, coconut milk, and lime juice in a zippered freezer bag.
2. Season with salt and pepper then shake to coat and marinate for 30 minutes in the refrigerator.
3. Pour the bag into the Instant Pot then add the tomatoes, onion, carrots, butter, and curry powder.
4. Close and lock the lid then press the Manual button and adjust the timer to 20 minutes.
5. When the timer goes off, allow the steam to vent naturally for 15 minutes then press the Cancel button and switch the steam release valve to the "venting" position to Quick Release the remaining steam.
6. When the float valve drops down, unlock and open the lid.
7. Stir in the zucchini then press the Sauté button – cook for 5 minutes, stirring occasionally, until the sauce is thickened.
8. Adjust seasoning to taste then spoon over rice and serve with fresh cilantro.

Nutrition: 325 calories per serving, 15.5g fat, 34.4g protein, 12.5g carbs, 3.7g fiber

Hearty Beef Stroganoff

Yield: makes 6 servings

Prep Time: 15 minutes

Cook Time: 17 minutes

In the Pot Time: 45 minutes

Total Time: 1 hour

Function Buttons: Sauté (More), Manual

Ingredients:

- 2 tablespoons olive oil
- 2 pounds beef stew meat, chopped
- Salt and pepper
- 8 ounces sliced mushrooms
- 1 medium yellow onion, chopped
- 1 tablespoon minced garlic
- 1 teaspoon fresh chopped thyme
- 2 tablespoons all-purpose flour
- ¼ cup dry cooking sherry
- 3 cups beef broth
- 1 tablespoon Worcestershire sauce
- 12 ounces egg noodles
- 1 cup sour cream

Instructions:

1. Press the Sauté button on the Instant Pot and adjust it to More then wait for the display to read "hot."
2. Add the oil and let it heat up while you season the beef with salt and pepper.
3. Place the beef in the pot and cook until browned, stirring occasionally, about 3 to 4 minutes.
4. Spoon the beef into a bowl then add the mushrooms, onion, garlic, and thyme to the pot.
5. Cook for 3 to 4 minutes, stirring occasionally, until tender.
6. Stir in the flour and cook for 1 minute then stir in the sherry, scraping the browned bits from the bottom of the pot.
7. Add the beef broth and Worcestershire as well as the browned beef.
8. Close and lock the lid then press the Manual button and adjust the timer to 12 minutes.
9. When the timer goes off, press the Cancel button and switch the steam release valve to the "venting" position to Quick Release the steam.
10. When the float valve drops down, unlock and open the lid.
11. Stir in the noodles then close and lock the lid then press the Manual button and adjust the timer to 5 minutes.
12. When the timer goes off, press the Cancel button and switch the steam release valve to the "venting" position to Quick Release the steam.
13. When the float valve drops down, unlock and open the lid.
14. Stir in the sour cream then season with salt and pepper and serve hot.

Nutrition: 540 calories per serving, 24.2g fat, 53.9g protein, 22.7g carbs, 1.6g fiber

Lamb and Sweet Potato Stew

Yield: makes 4 servings

Prep Time: 15 minutes

Cook Time: 35 minutes

In the Pot Time: 1 hour 15 minutes

Total Time: 1 hour 50 minutes

Function Buttons: Sauté, Sauté (Less), Manual

Ingredients:

- 1 tablespoon olive oil
- 1 ½ pounds boneless lamb shoulder, chopped
- ½ tablespoon ground coriander
- 1 teaspoon ground cumin
- Salt and pepper
- 1 medium yellow onion, chopped
- 2 tablespoons fresh grated ginger
- 1 tablespoon minced garlic
- 1 tablespoon tomato paste
- 1 cup beef broth
- 1 (2-inch) cinnamon stick
- 2 large sweet potatoes, cut into cubes
- Fresh chopped cilantro

Instructions:

1. Press the Sauté button on the Instant Pot and wait for the display to read "hot."
2. Add the oil and let it heat up while you toss the lamb with the spices.
3. Place the lamb in the pot and cook until browned, stirring occasionally, about 6 minutes.
4. Spoon the lamb into a bowl and reduce the Sauté to Less.
5. Add the onion and sauté for 3 to 4 minutes until the onion is translucent then stir in the ginger, garlic, and tomato paste.
6. Cook for 1 minute, stirring often, then stir in the broth and cinnamon.
7. Add the lamb back to the pot then close and lock the lid.
8. Press the Manual button and adjust the timer to 25 minutes.
9. When the timer goes off, allow the steam to vent naturally and, when the float valve drops down, unlock and open the lid.
10. Stir in the sweet potatoes then close and lock the lid.
11. Press the Manual button and adjust the timer to 10 minutes.
12. When the timer goes off, press the Cancel button and switch the steam release valve to the "venting" position to Quick Release the steam.
13. When the float valve drops down, unlock and open the lid.
14. Stir everything well and adjust seasoning to taste before serving over steamed rice, garnished with fresh chopped cilantro.

Nutrition: 500 calories per serving, 16.8g fat, 51.4g protein, 34.4g carbs, 5.2g fiber

Pork and Poultry Recipes

Recipes Included in this Chapter:

- Turkey-Stuffed Bell Peppers
- Brown Sugar Balsamic Pork Tenderloin
- Chicken and Rice Burrito Bowl
- Pork Loin with Veggies and Gravy
- Indian Butter Chicken
- Carnitas with Pickled Onion
- Turkey Breast with Gravy
- Easy Chicken Adobo
- Honey BBQ Pulled Pork
- Whole Chicken with Mushrooms
- Cuban Pork with Rice and Beans
- Chicken Cacciatore
- Ginger Soy Pork Tenderloin
- Coconut Braised Pork Shoulder

Turkey-Stuffed Bell Peppers

Yield: makes 4 servings

Prep Time: 10 minutes

Cook Time: 15 minutes

In the Pot Time: 40 minutes

Total Time: 50 minutes

Function Buttons: Manual

Ingredients:

- 1 pound lean ground turkey (93% lean)
- 1 cup steamed brown rice
- ¼ cup plain breadcrumbs
- ¼ cup diced red onion
- ¼ cup grated parmesan cheese
- 2 tablespoons fresh chopped parsley
- 1 tablespoon tomato paste
- ¾ cup marinara sauce, divided
- 1 large egg
- Salt and pepper
- ½ cup water
- ¼ cup shredded mozzarella cheese

Instructions:

1. Stir together the ground turkey, brown rice, breadcrumbs, onion, parmesan cheese, and parsley in a mixing bowl.
2. Add the tomato paste, ¼ cup marinara sauce, and the egg – season with salt and pepper.
3. Slice the tops off the peppers then remove the seeds and pith.
4. Place the steamer insert in the Instant Pot and pour in the water.
5. Spoon the turkey mixture into the peppers then place them in the Instant Pot on the steamer rack.
6. Spoon the remaining marinara sauce over the peppers then close and lock the lid.
7. Press the Manual button and adjust the timer to 15 minutes.
8. When the timer goes off, allow the steam to vent naturally and, when the float valve drops down, unlock and open the lid.
9. Sprinkle the cheese over the peppers then close the lid until it melts. Serve hot.

Nutrition: 350 calories per serving, 13.5g fat, 29.9g protein, 27.2g carbs, 2.5g fiber

Brown Sugar Balsamic Pork Tenderloin

Yield: makes 6 servings

Prep Time: 10 minutes

Cook Time: 35 minutes

In the Pot Time: 1 hour

Total Time: 1 hour 10 minutes

Function Buttons: Sauté, Meat/Stew

Ingredients:

- ¼ cup balsamic vinegar
- ¼ cup warm water
- ¼ cup brown sugar, packed
- 4 cloves minced garlic
- 1 tablespoon cornstarch
- 1 tablespoon soy sauce
- 2 tablespoons olive oil
- 1 (2-pound) pork tenderloin, cut into pieces

Instructions:

1. Whisk together the balsamic vinegar, water, brown sugar, garlic, cornstarch, and soy sauce in a small bowl.
2. Press the Sauté button on the Instant Pot and wait for the display to read "hot."
3. Add the oil and season the pork with salt and pepper while it heats up.
4. Place the pork in the Instant Pot and cook to brown on all sides – about 6 to 8 minutes.
5. Pour in the sauce then close and lock the lid.
6. Press the Meat/Stew button and adjust the timer to 35 minutes.
7. When the timer goes off, allow the steam to vent naturally and, when the float valve drops down, unlock and open the lid. Remove the pork and serve hot.

Nutrition: 290 calories per serving, 10g fat, 39.9g protein, 8.1g carbs, 0.1g fiber

Chicken and Rice Burrito Bowl

Yield: makes 6 servings

Prep Time: 10 minutes

Cook Time: 10 minutes

In the Pot Time: 25 minutes

Total Time: 35 minutes

Function Buttons: Sauté, Manual

Ingredients:

- 2 tablespoons olive oil
- 1 medium yellow onion, chopped
- 3 cloves minced garlic
- 1 tablespoon chili powder
- 2 teaspoons ground cumin
- 1 cup chicken broth, divided
- 1 ½ pounds boneless chicken thighs, chopped
- Salt and pepper
- 1 (16-ounce) jar mild salsa
- 1 (15-ounce) can black beans, rinsed and drained
- 1 cup frozen corn
- 1 cup long-grain rice, uncooked

Instructions:

1. Press the Sauté button on the Instant Pot and wait for the display to read "hot."
2. Add the oil and wait for it to heat up then stir in the onions and garlic.
3. Sauté the onions until translucent, about 4 minutes, then stir in the chili powder and cumin.
4. Cook for another 30 seconds then stir in ¼ cup of the chicken broth.
5. Scrape up the browned bits from the bottom of the pot and let simmer for 1 minute.
6. Season the chicken with salt and pepper then add it to the pot along with the salsa, beans, and corn – stir well.
7. Add the rice to the pot along with the remaining chicken broth – do not stir.
8. Close and lock the lid then press the Manual button and adjust the timer to 10 minutes.
9. When the timer goes off, press the Cancel button and switch the steam release valve to the "venting" position to Quick Release the steam.
10. When the float valve drops down, unlock and open the lid.
11. Stir everything well then spoon into bowls and top with shredded cheese and fresh cilantro.

Nutrition: 490 calories per serving, 23.2g fat, 27.1g protein, 41.4g carbs, 3.7g fiber

Pork Loin with Veggies and Gravy

Yield: makes 6 servings

Prep Time: 10 minutes

Cook Time: 30 minutes

In the Pot Time: 50 minutes

Total Time: 1 hour

Function Buttons: Sauté, Manual

Ingredients:

- 2 tablespoons butter
- 1 (2-pound) boneless pork tenderloin
- Salt and pepper
- 1 small yellow onion, chopped
- 3 cloves minced garlic
- 2 large carrots, peeled and chopped
- 2 stalks celery, peeled and chopped
- ½ cup chicken broth
- 2 tablespoons Worcestershire sauce
- 1 tablespoon brown sugar
- 1 tablespoon Dijon mustard
- 1 tablespoon dried rosemary
- 1 teaspoon dried basil
- 1 teaspoon dried oregano
- 1/4 cup cold water
- 1 tablespoon cornstarch

Instructions:

1. Press the Sauté button on the Instant Pot and wait for the display to read "hot."
2. Add the butter to the pot and let it melt while you season the pork with salt and pepper.
3. Place the pork in the pot and cook to sear on all sides, turning as needed, about 6 to 8 minutes.
4. Add the onions and garlic then cook for 2 minutes.
5. Stir in the carrots and celery along with the chicken broth, Worcestershire sauce, brown sugar, and mustard.
6. Sprinkle in the herbs then close and lock the lid.
7. Press the Manual button and adjust the timer to 30 minutes.
8. When the timer goes off, press the Cancel button and switch the steam release valve to the "venting" position to Quick Release the steam.
9. When the float valve drops down, unlock and open the lid.
10. Check to make sure the pork is cooked to 145°F then remove it to a cutting board.
11. Cover the pork loosely with foil and let rest for 10 minutes while you prepare the gravy.
12. Whisk together the cornstarch and water then stir it into the cooking liquid.
13. Press the Sauté button and simmer until the gravy thickens then season with salt and pepper to taste. Slice the pork and serve with the gravy and vegetables.

Nutrition: 235 calories per serving, 8.1g fat, 29g protein, 9.6g carbs, 1.2g fiber

Indian Butter Chicken

Yield: makes 4 servings

Prep Time: 10 minutes

Cook Time: 10 minutes

In the Pot Time: 35 minutes

Total Time: 45 minutes

Function Buttons: Sauté, Manual

Ingredients:

- 2 tablespoons ghee or olive oil
- 1 large yellow onion, chopped
- 1 ½ tablespoons fresh grated ginger
- 1 tablespoon minced garlic
- 1 tablespoon garam masala
- 1 ¼ teaspoon ground coriander
- 1 teaspoon ground turmeric
- Salt and pepper
- 2 pounds boneless skinless chicken thighs
- 2 (14-ounce) cans diced tomatoes in juice
- ½ cup heavy cream

Instructions:

1. Press the Sauté button on the Instant Pot and wait for the display to read "hot."
2. Add the ghee and let it heat up then stir in the onion, ginger, garlic, and spices.
3. Sauté for 5 minutes then add the chicken and diced tomatoes.
4. Close and lock the lid then press the Manual button and adjust the timer to 10 minutes.
5. When the timer goes off, allow the steam to vent naturally for 10 minutes then switch the steam release valve to the "venting" position to Quick Release the remaining steam.
6. When the float valve drops down, unlock and open the lid.
7. Remove the chicken to a serving bowl with a slotted spoon.
8. Puree the sauce in the Instant Pot using an immersion blender then stir in the cream.
9. Cut the chicken into chunks then stir it back into the pot. Serve over steamed rice.

Nutrition: 615 calories per serving, 29.5g fat, 68.1g protein, 15.4g carbs, 2.5g fiber

Carnitas with Pickled Onion

Yield: makes 8 servings

Prep Time: 10 minutes

Cook Time: 40 minutes

In the Pot Time: 1 hour 10 minutes

Total Time: 1 hour 20 minutes

Function Buttons: Manual

Ingredients:

- 1 medium red onion, sliced thin
- ½ cup apple cider vinegar
- ¼ cup fresh lime juice
- 3 tablespoons sugar
- Pinch red pepper flakes
- 1 tablespoon ground cumin
- 1 tablespoon garlic salt
- 2 teaspoons dried oregano
- 2 teaspoons brown sugar
- 1 ½ teaspoons chili powder
- 1 teaspoon paprika
- 1 teaspoon coriander
- 5 pounds boneless pork shoulder, cut into 2-inch pieces
- 1 cup water
- Juice from 2 oranges
- Juice from ½ lemon
- Salt, as needed

Instructions:

1. Place the onions in a bowl then pour boiling water over them – soak for 10 seconds then drain.
2. Whisk together the vinegar, lime juice, sugar, and red pepper flakes along with ½ tablespoon salt in a small saucepan.
3. Heat over medium heat for 2 to 3 minutes until the sugar dissolves.
4. Pour the mixture over the onions then set aside to cool – when cooled, transfer to the refrigerator.
5. Stir together the cumin, garlic salt, oregano, brown sugar, chili powder, paprika, and coriander in a small bowl.
6. Rub the spice mixture into the pork then place it in the Instant Pot.
7. Add the water, orange juice, and lemon juice then close and lock the lid.
8. Press the Manual button and adjust the timer to 40 minutes.
9. When the timer goes off, allow the steam to vent naturally for 15 minutes then switch the steam release valve to the "venting" position to Quick Release the remaining steam.
10. When the float valve drops down, unlock and open the lid.
11. Remove the pork to a foil-lined baking sheet with a slotted spoon.
12. Shred the pork and season with salt then broil for 3 to 5 minutes until browned.
13. Serve the pork on warmed tortillas with the pickled onions and your favorite taco toppings.

Nutrition: 450 calories per serving, 10.4g fat, 74.9g protein, 10.2g carbs, 1g fiber

Turkey Breast with Gravy

Yield: makes 8 servings

Prep Time: 25 minutes (including rest time)

Cook Time: 25 minutes

In the Pot Time: 50 minutes

Total Time: 1 hour 15 minutes

Function Buttons: Sauté (More), Manual

Ingredients:

- 1 tablespoon coconut oil
- 1 tablespoon paprika
- 1 tablespoon dried Italian seasoning
- 1 teaspoon dried oregano
- Salt and pepper
- 1 (4-pound) turkey breast
- 2 tablespoons olive oil
- 2 tablespoons butter
- ½ cup chicken broth
- ½ cup whole milk

Instructions:

1. Press the Sauté button on the Instant Pot then adjust to More and wait for the display to read "hot."
2. Rub the turkey with coconut oil then sprinkle with paprika, Italian seasoning, and oregano.
3. Season with salt and pepper, rubbing the spices into the turkey skin.
4. Add the olive oil to the pot then let it heat up – add the turkey to the Instant Pot and sprinkle with garlic.
5. Cook for 2 minutes on each side until browned all around, about 6 to 8 minutes.
6. Remove the turkey to a plate then place the steamer rack inside the Instant Pot.
7. Place the turkey on top of the rack then close and lock the lid.
8. Press the Manual button and adjust the timer to 25 minutes.
9. When the timer goes off, allow the steam to vent naturally and, when the float valve drops down, unlock and open the lid.
10. Transfer the turkey to a cutting board and tent loosely with foil – let rest for 10 to 15 minutes before slicing.
11. Meanwhile, turn the Instant Pot back to the Sauté setting and adjust to More.
12. Add the butter to the cooking liquid then whisk in the flour.
13. Simmer for 2 minutes while stirring constantly then whisk in the chicken broth and milk – cook for 3 minutes until thickened.
14. Serve the turkey hot drizzled with gravy.

Nutrition: 320 calories per serving, 12.6g fat, 39.7g protein, 10.9g carbs, 1.5g fiber

Easy Chicken Adobo

Yield: makes 4 servings

Prep Time: 20 minutes

Cook Time: 15 minutes

In the Pot Time: 40 minutes

Total Time: 1 hour

Function Buttons: Sauté, Manual

Ingredients:

- 2 pounds bone-in chicken thighs
- Salt and pepper
- ¾ cup apple cider vinegar
- ¼ cup soy sauce
- 2 tablespoons minced garlic
- 2 small bay leaves

Instructions:

1. Season the chicken with salt and pepper then place it skin-side down in the Instant Pot.
2. Pour in the cider vinegar and soy sauce then add the garlic and bay leaves.
3. Close and lock the lid then press the Manual button and adjust the timer to 15 minutes.
4. When the timer goes off, allow the steam to vent naturally and, when the float valve drops down, unlock and open the lid.
5. Transfer the chicken to a foil-lined baking sheet and set it aside.
6. Press the Sauté button on the Instant Pot and wait for the display panel to read "hot."
7. Set the timer for 10 minutes and stir the sauce occasionally as it thickens.
8. Broil the chicken under the broiler until browned, turning the baking sheet once after 2 to 3 minutes.
9. Transfer the chicken to a serving plate.
10. Remove and discard the bay leaf then adjust the seasoning to taste for the sauce.
11. Serve the chicken hot over steamed rice with the adobo sauce.

Nutrition: 505 calories per serving, 34.1g fat, 41.3g protein, 3.3g carbs, 0.3g fiber

Honey BBQ Pulled Pork

Yield: makes 6 servings

Prep Time: 10 minutes

Cook Time: 40 minutes

In the Pot Time: 1 hour

Total Time: 1 hour 10 minutes

Function Buttons: Sauté, Manual

Ingredients:

- 2 tablespoons brown sugar, packed
- 1 tablespoon garlic powder
- 1 tablespoon onion powder
- 2 teaspoons paprika
- 1 teaspoon ground cumin
- Salt and pepper
- 1 (3-pound) boneless pork roast, cut into chunks
- 1 ½ cups barbecue sauce
- 1 ¼ cup chicken broth, divided
- 1/3 cup apple cider vinegar
- 2 tablespoons honey
- 2 tablespoons olive oil

Instructions:

1. Whisk together the brown sugar, garlic powder, onion powder, paprika, cumin, salt and pepper in a small bowl.
2. Rub the spice mixture into the pork roast then set it aside.
3. Whisk together the barbecue sauce, 1 cup chicken broth, the honey, and the cider vinegar in a bowl then set aside.
4. Press the Sauté button on the Instant Pot and wait for the display to read "hot."
5. Add the oil and, when it is hot, add the pork to the Instant Pot.
6. Cook the pork for 4 to 5 minutes, stirring occasionally until browned then remove to a bowl using a slotted spoon – cook in two batches, if necessary.
7. Pour the remaining chicken broth into the pot and stir to loosen the browned bits from the bottom of the pot.
8. Add the pork back to the pot and pour in the sauce.
9. Close and lock the lid then press the Manual button and adjust the timer to 40 minutes.
10. When the timer goes off, allow the steam to vent naturally for 10 minutes then switch the steam release valve to the "venting" position to Quick Release the remaining steam.
11. When the float valve drops down, unlock and open the lid.
12. Shred the pork with two for ks and stir it into the sauce then serve on toasted sandwich buns with your favorite sandwich toppings.

Nutrition: 505 calories per serving, 13.3g fat, 60.7g protein, 31.7g carbs, 0.8g fiber

Rotisserie-Style Whole Chicken

Yield: makes 8 servings

Prep Time: 15 minutes

Cook Time: 24 minutes

In the Pot Time: 50 minutes

Total Time: 1 hour 5 minutes

Function Buttons: Sauté, Manual

Ingredients:

- 1 ½ tablespoons dried Italian seasoning
- 1 tablespoon salt
- ½ tablespoon smoked paprika
- 1 teaspoon garlic powder
- ½ teaspoon onion powder
- ½ teaspoon pepper
- 2 tablespoons olive oil, divided
- 1 (6-pound) whole chicken
- 1 medium onion, quartered
- 1 lemon, cut in half
- 3 cloves garlic, peeled
- 2 tablespoons butter
- 1 cup chicken broth

Instructions:

1. Combine the Italian seasoning, salt, pepper, paprika, garlic powder, and onion powder in a small bowl.
2. Loosen the skin and rub a tablespoon of olive oil plus 1/3 of the spice mixture under it.
3. Rub another tablespoon of olive oil on top of the skin along with the rest of the seasonings.
4. Place the onion, lemon, and garlic in the chicken cavity.
5. Press the Sauté button on the Instant Pot and wait for the display to read "hot."
6. Add the butter to the pot and let it melt then place the chicken skin-side down in the pot.
7. Cook for 6 to 7 minutes to sear then turn the chicken and cook for another 5 minutes.
8. Remove the chicken to a cutting board then place a trivet inside the pot.
9. Pour in the chicken broth then place the chicken on top of the trivet.
10. Close and lock the lid then press the Manual button and adjust the timer to 24 minutes.
11. When the timer goes off, allow the steam to vent naturally for 15 minutes then switch the steam release valve to the "venting" position to Quick Release the remaining steam.
12. When the float valve drops down, unlock and open the lid.
13. Transfer the chicken to a cutting board and cool for 5 to 10 minutes before carving to serve.

Nutrition: 490 calories per serving, 34.6g fat, 43g protein, 2.5g carbs, 0.5g fiber

Cuban Pork with Rice and Beans

Yield: makes 4 servings

Prep Time: 10 minutes

Cook Time: 12 minutes

In the Pot Time: 30 minutes

Total Time: 40 minutes

Function Buttons: Sauté, Manual

Ingredients:

- 2 tablespoons olive oil
- 1 (1 ½-pound) boneless pork tenderloin
- Salt and pepper
- 1 ¼ cups chicken broth
- ½ cup orange juice, fresh squeezed
- 1 ½ tablespoons minced garlic
- 2 tablespoons taco seasoning
- 1 teaspoon ground cumin
- 1 (15-ounce) can black beans, rinsed and drained
- 1 cup long-grain white rice, uncooked
- 1 to 2 tablespoons fresh lime juice

Instructions:

1. Press the Sauté button on the Instant Pot and wait for the display to read "hot."
2. Add the oil to the pot and let it heat up while you season the pork with salt and pepper.
3. Place the pork in the pot and cook for 5 minutes, stirring occasionally, until browned.
4. Add the chicken broth, orange juice, garlic, taco seasoning, and cumin.
5. Stir in the beans and rice then close and lock the lid.
6. Press the Manual button and adjust the timer to 12 minutes.
7. When the timer goes off, press the Cancel button and switch the steam release valve to the "venting" position to Quick Release the steam.
8. When the float valve drops down, unlock and open the lid.
9. Stir in the lime juice then spoon into bowls and serve with fresh cilantro.

Nutrition: 560 calories per serving, 16.5g fat, 45g protein, 56.1g carbs, 4.6g fiber

Chicken Cacciatore

Yield: makes 4 servings

Prep Time: 5 minutes

Cook Time: 15 minutes

In the Pot Time: 40 minutes

Total Time: 45 minutes

Function Buttons: Sauté, Manual

Ingredients:

- 1 cup chicken broth
- 1 medium bay leaf
- 1 teaspoon salt
- 2 pounds bone-in chicken drumsticks
- 1 medium yellow onion, chopped
- 1 teaspoon garlic powder
- 1 teaspoon dried oregano
- 2 (14-ounce) cans stewed tomatoes
- ½ cup black olives

Instructions:

1. Press the Sauté button on the Instant Pot and wait for the display to read "hot."
2. Pour in the chicken broth then add the bay leaf and salt.
3. Add the chicken, onions, garlic powder, and oregano then pour in the tomatoes.
4. Close and lock the lid then press the Manual button and adjust the timer to 15 minutes.
5. When the timer goes off, allow the steam to vent naturally and, when the float valve drops down, unlock and open the lid.
6. Discard the bay leaf and stir the ingredients well. Serve hot garnished with black olives, if desired.

Nutrition: 420 calories per serving, 20.6g fat, 45.6g protein, 12.4g carbs, 3.8g fiber

Ginger Soy Pork Tenderloin

Yield: makes 4 servings

Prep Time: 10 minutes

Cook Time: 5 minutes

In the Pot Time: 25 minutes

Total Time: 35 minutes

Function Buttons: Manual, Sauté

Ingredients:

- ½ cup soy sauce
- ¼ cup water
- ¼ cup brown sugar
- 2 tablespoons fresh grated ginger
- 1 teaspoon minced garlic
- 1 tablespoon sesame oil
- 1 (1-pound) boneless pork tenderloin
- Salt and pepper
- 1 tablespoon cornstarch
- 1 tablespoons cold water

Instructions:

1. Combine the soy sauce, water, brown sugar, ginger, garlic, and sesame oil in the pot of your Instant Pot.
2. Stir well then season the pork with salt and pepper then add it to the pot.
3. Close and lock the lid then press the Manual button and adjust the timer to 5 minutes.
4. When the timer goes off, allow the steam to vent naturally for 7 minutes then switch the steam release valve to the "venting" position to Quick Release the remaining steam.
5. When the float valve drops down, unlock and open the lid.
6. Remove the pork to a cutting board then whisk together the cornstarch and water then pour it into the pot.
7. Stir well and press the Sauté button – cook until thickened.
8. Slice the pork and serve drizzled with the ginger soy sauce.

Nutrition: 260 calories per serving, 7.4g fat, 31.7g protein, 14.9g carbs, 0.3g fiber

Coconut Braised Pork Shoulder

Yield: makes 8 servings

Prep Time: 15 minutes

Cook Time: 55 minutes

In the Pot Time: 1 hour 15 minutes

Total Time: 1 hour 30 minutes

Function Buttons: Sauté, Manual

Ingredients:

- 2 tablespoons olive oil
- 1 (4-pound) boneless pork shoulder, cut into pieces
- Salt and pepper
- 1 large yellow onion, chopped
- 2 tablespoons sliced ginger
- 1 tablespoon minced garlic
- 1 cup chicken broth
- 3 cups sliced green cabbage
- 1 tablespoon grated lemon zest
- 2 ½ cups unsweetened coconut milk (from a carton)
- 1 ¼ teaspoon ground cumin
- 1 teaspoon curry powder
- ¼ to ½ teaspoon chili flakes

Instructions:

1. Press the Sauté button on the Instant Pot and wait for the display to read "hot."
2. Add the olive oil then let it heat up while you season the pork with salt and pepper.
3. Place the pork in the pot and cook until browned on all sides, turning as needed – about 6 to 8 minutes.
4. Remove the pork to a cutting board and add the onions, ginger, and garlic to the pot.
5. Cook until the onions are translucent, about 3 minutes, then stir in the chicken broth and scrape up the browned bits from the bottom of the pot.
6. Add the pork back to the pot along with the cabbage, lemon, and coconut milk.
7. Sprinkle in the cumin, curry powder, and chili flakes.
8. Close and lock the lid then press the Manual button and adjust to More than set the timer to 55 minutes.
9. When the timer goes off, press the Cancel button and switch the steam release valve to the "venting" position to Quick Release the steam.
10. When the float valve drops down, unlock and open the lid.
11. Remove the pork to a cutting board and cut into chunks then return to the pot.
12. Adjust seasoning to taste and serve hot over steamed rice.

Nutrition: 550 calories per serving, 29.7g fat, 62.5g protein, 8.7g carbs, 2.9g fiber

Soups, Stews, and Chilis

Recipes Included in this Chapter:

- Beefy Bacon Chili
- Hearty Clam Chowder
- Chipotle Chicken Sweet Potato Chili
- Easy French Onion Soup
- Curried Beef Stew
- Classic Minestrone
- Vegan Black Bean Chili
- Chicken Tortilla Soup
- Navy Bean and Ham Soup
- Broccoli Cheddar Soup
- White Bean Chicken Chili
- Spinach and Brown Lentil Soup
- Butternut Squash Beef Stew
- Creamy Lobster Bisque

Beefy Bacon Chili

Yield: makes 4 servings

Prep Time: 15 minutes

Cook Time: 30 minutes

In the Pot Time: 50 minutes

Total Time: 1 hour 5 minutes

Function Buttons: Sauté, Bean/Chili

Ingredients:

- 6 slices bacon, chopped
- 1 medium yellow onion, chopped
- 2 red bell peppers, diced
- 2 cloves minced garlic
- 1 pound lean beef (90% lean)
- 1 (14-ounce) can roasted diced tomatoes
- 1 (8-ounce) can tomato sauce
- 1 tablespoon chili powder
- 1 tablespoon smoked paprika
- 1 tablespoon garlic powder
- ½ tablespoon ground cumin
- ¼ to ½ teaspoon cayenne
- Salt and pepper
- Diced avocado, to serve
- Sour cream, to serve

Instructions:

1. Press the Sauté button on the Instant Pot then add the bacon.
2. Cook the bacon until it is crisp then spoon it into a bowl using a slotted spoon.
3. Stir the onions, peppers, and garlic into the bacon fat and sauté for 5 minutes.
4. Add the beef, tomatoes, tomato sauce, and the seasonings and stir well.
5. Sauté for another 5 minutes then stir the cooked bacon into the pot.
6. Close and lock the lid then press the Bean/Chili button – it will automatically cook for 30 minutes.
7. When the timer goes off, allow the steam to vent naturally for 10 minutes then switch the steam release valve to the "venting" position to Quick Release the remaining steam.
8. When the float valve drops down, unlock and open the lid.
9. Stir the chili well then spoon into bowls and serve with diced avocado and sour cream.

Nutrition: 405 calories per serving, 20.2g fat, 37.9g protein, 18.2g carbs, 4.8g fiber

Hearty Clam Chowder

Yield: makes 6 servings

Prep Time: 5 minutes

Cook Time: 5 minutes

In the Pot Time: 25 minutes

Total Time: 30 minutes

Function Buttons: Sauté, Manual, Sauté (Less)

Ingredients:

- 3 (6.5-ounce) cans chopped clams
- Water, as needed
- 4 slices bacon, chopped
- 3 tablespoons butter
- 1 medium yellow onion, chopped
- 2 medium stalks celery, diced
- ¼ teaspoon dried thyme
- 2 cloves minced garlic
- Salt and pepper
- 4 cups diced Yukon gold potatoes
- 1 ¼ cups half-n-half

Instructions:

1. Drain the canned clams into a large glass measuring cup.
2. Add enough water to make 2 cups of liquid then set it and the drained clams aside.
3. Press the Sauté button on the Instant Pot and wait for the display panel to read "hot."
4. Add the bacon to the Instant Pot and cook until the fat renders, stirring often.
5. Stir in the butter, diced onion, celery, and thyme.
6. Cook for 2 minutes, stirring often, loosening the browned bits from the bottom of the pot.
7. Stir in the garlic then season with salt and pepper then cook for 1 minute.
8. Add the potatoes along with the clam juice mixture then stir well.

9. Close and lock the lid then press the Manual button and set the timer for 5 minutes.
10. When the timer goes off, let the pressure vent naturally for 3 minutes before pressing the Cancel button.
11. Switch the steam release valve to the "venting" position to Quick Release the remaining pressure.
12. When the float valve drops down, unlock and open the lid.
13. Use a potato masher to mash some of the potatoes then press the Sauté button and adjust it to Less.
14. Stir in the clams and half-n-half then let it cook until just heated through. Serve hot.

Nutrition: 230 calories per serving, 14.5g fat, 10.8g protein, 14.2g carbs, 1.6g fiber

Chipotle Chicken Sweet Potato Chili

Yield: makes 4 servings

Prep Time: 10 minutes

Cook Time: 12 minutes

In the Pot Time: 35 minutes

Total Time: 45 minutes

Function Buttons: Sauté, Manual

Ingredients:

- 1 tablespoon olive oil
- 1 medium red onion, diced
- 2 cloves minced garlic
- 2 tablespoons chipotle chili powder
- 1 teaspoon ground cumin
- Salt to taste
- 2 cups diced sweet potato
- 1 (15-ounce) can black beans, drained
- 1 (14-ounce) can diced tomatoes
- 1 cup frozen corn
- 1 pound boneless skinless chicken thighs
- 1 cup chicken broth

Instructions:

1. Press the Sauté button then add the oil to the Instant Pot and wait for the display panel to read "hot."
2. Add the onions and cook for 3 minutes until translucent then stir in the garlic.
3. Cook for 1 minute then add the chipotle chili powder, cumin, and salt.
4. Add the sweet potato, black beans, diced tomatoes, and corn then stir well.
5. Place the chicken on top then pour in the chicken broth.
6. Close and lock the lid then press the Manual button and adjust the timer to 12 minutes.
7. When the timer goes off, allow the steam to vent naturally and, when the float valve drops down, unlock and open the lid.
8. Shred the chicken with two forks then spoon the chili into bowls.
9. Serve hot with sliced avocado, shredded cheese, and sour cream.

Nutrition: 465 calories per serving, 14.1g fat, 41.7g protein, 44.8g carbs, 9.7g fiber

Easy French Onion Soup

Yield: makes 4 servings

Prep Time: 15 minutes

Cook Time: 10 minutes

In the Pot Time: 30 minutes

Total Time: 45 minutes

Function Buttons: Sauté, Manual

Ingredients:

- 2 tablespoons olive oil
- 2 tablespoons butter
- 4 large yellow onions, sliced
- 5 cups vegetable broth
- 2 small bay leaves
- 1 teaspoon dried thyme
- Salt and pepper
- 4 thick slices French baguette
- 4 slices provolone cheese

Instructions:

1. Press the Sauté button on the Instant Pot and wait for the display to read "hot."
2. Add the oil and butter – let it heat for a few seconds then stir in the onion.
3. Cook the onions for 4 to 5 minutes until browned then stir in the vegetable broth.
4. Scrape up the browned bits from the bottom of the pot then stir in the bay leaves, thyme, salt, and pepper.
5. Close and lock the lid then press the Manual button and adjust the timer to 10 minutes.
6. When the timer goes off, allow the steam to vent naturally and, when the float valve drops down, unlock and open the lid.
7. While waiting for the pressure to vent, preheat the broiler in your oven and toast the slices of baguette on a baking sheet until browned.
8. Spoon the soup into bowls and add a slice of toasted baguette to each.
9. Top each bowl with a slice of cheese then broil until browned and serve hot.

Nutrition: 450 calories per serving, 22.1g fat, 19g protein, 44.2g carbs, 4.4g fiber

Curried Beef Stew

Yield: makes 6 servings

Prep Time: 15 minutes

Cook Time: 30 minutes

In the Pot Time: 45 minutes

Total Time: 1 hour

Function Buttons: Sauté, Meat/Stew

Ingredients:

- 2 tablespoons butter or ghee
- 1 large yellow onion, chopped
- 4 cloves minced garlic
- 1 pound beef sirloin, cut into chunks
- 3 large Yukon gold potatoes, cut into chunks
- 4 large carrots, peeled and sliced
- 1 cup canned coconut milk
- ½ cup beef broth
- 2 tablespoons curry powder
- 1 teaspoon dried oregano
- ½ teaspoon paprika
- Salt and pepper

Instructions:

1. Press the Sauté button on the Instant Pot and wait for the display to read "hot."
2. Add the butter and let it melt then stir in the onions and garlic.
3. Sauté for 2 minutes then add the beef and cook until it is browned, stirring as needed, about 5 minutes more.
4. Press the Cancel button then add the potatoes, carrots, coconut milk, broth, curry powder, oregano, and paprika.
5. Season with salt and pepper then close and lock the lid.
6. Press the Meat/Stew button and adjust the timer to 30 minutes.
7. When the timer goes off, allow the steam to vent naturally and, when the float valve drops down, unlock and open the lid.
8. Spoon the stew over steamed rice or noodles.

Nutrition: 450 calories per serving, 18.8g fat, 28.6g protein, 43g carbs, 6.7g fiber

Classic Minestrone

Yield: makes 4 servings

Prep Time: 10 minutes

Cook Time: 6 minutes

In the Pot Time: 25 minutes

Total Time: 35 minutes

Function Buttons: Sauté, Manual

Ingredients:

- 2 tablespoons olive oil
- 2 large stalks celery, diced
- 1 large carrot, peeled and diced
- 1 large yellow onion, diced
- 3 cloves minced garlic
- Salt and pepper
- 1 ¼ teaspoon dried oregano
- ¾ teaspoon dried basil
- 4 cups vegetable broth
- 2 (14-ounce) cans diced tomatoes
- 1 (15-ounce) can white kidney beans
- 1 cup fresh baby spinach
- 1 cup elbow pasta
- Parmesan cheese, to serve
- Fresh chopped parsley

Instructions:

1. Press the Sauté button on the Instant Pot and wait for the display to read "hot."
2. Add the olive oil then stir in the celery, carrot, and onion.
3. Cook for 3 minutes until the onion is translucent then stir in the garlic and season with salt and pepper – cook for 30 seconds.
4. Stir in the oregano and basil then add the vegetable broth, tomatoes, beans, spinach, and pasta.
5. Close and lock the lid then press the Manual button and adjust the timer to 6 minutes.
6. When the timer goes off, allow the steam to vent naturally for 2 minutes then switch the steam release valve to the "venting" position to Quick Release the remaining steam.
7. When the float valve drops down, unlock and open the lid.
8. Spoon the soup into bowls and serve with parmesan cheese and fresh parsley.

Nutrition: 325 calories per serving, 9.5g fat, 14.8g protein, 45.9g carbs, 9.9g fiber

Vegan Black Bean Chili

Yield: makes 8 servings

Prep Time: 15 minutes

Cook Time: 5 minutes

In the Pot Time: 25 minutes

Total Time: 40 minutes

Function Buttons: Sauté, Manual

Ingredients:

- 1 tablespoon olive oil
- 1 large yellow onion, diced
- 1 small red pepper, diced
- 2 cloves minced garlic
- 1 teaspoon dried oregano
- 2 tablespoons chili powder
- ½ tablespoon ground cumin
- 2 (15-ounce) cans black beans, drained
- 1 (14.5-ounce) can fire-roasted tomatoes
- 1 jalapeno, seeded and minced
- 1 cup water
- Salt and pepper

Instructions:

1. Press the Sauté button on the Instant Pot and wait for the display to read "hot."
2. Add the olive oil then stir in the onions, peppers, garlic, and oregano.
3. Sauté for 6 to 7 minutes until browned then stir in the chili powder and cumin – cook for 1 minute more.
4. Stir in the beans, tomatoes, jalapeno, and water then season with salt and pepper.
5. Close and lock the lid then press the Manual button and adjust the timer to 5 minutes.
6. When the timer goes off, press the Cancel button and switch the steam release valve to the "venting" position to Quick Release the steam.
7. When the float valve drops down, unlock and open the lid.
8. Spoon into bowls and garnish with diced red onion and fresh cilantro to serve.

Nutrition: 400 calories per serving, 3.7g fat, 23.3g protein, 70.7g carbs, 17.5g fiber

Chicken Tortilla Soup

Yield: makes 6 servings

Prep Time: 10 minutes

Cook Time: 4 minutes

In the Pot Time: 20 minutes

Total Time: 30 minutes

Function Buttons: Sauté, Soup

Ingredients:

- 1 tablespoon olive oil
- 1 large yellow onion, chopped
- 2 (6-inch) corn tortillas, chopped into pieces
- 3 tablespoons fresh chopped cilantro
- 2 cloves minced garlic
- 1 large tomato, diced
- 1 (15-ounce) can black beans, drained
- 1 cup frozen corn
- 1 pound boneless skinless chicken thighs
- ½ tablespoon chili powder
- 1 teaspoon ground cumin
- ¼ teaspoon cayenne
- 3 ½ cups chicken broth

Instructions:

1. Press the Sauté button on the Instant Pot and wait for the display to read "hot."
2. Add the olive oil then stir in the onion and cook for 3 to 4 minutes until softened.
3. Stir in the chopped tortillas, cilantro, and garlic then cook for 1 minute.
4. Add the tomatoes, beans, corn, chicken, and spices along with the chicken broth.
5. Close and lock the lid then press the Soup button and adjust the timer to 4 minutes.
6. When the timer goes off, press the Cancel button and switch the steam release valve to the "venting" position to Quick Release the steam.
7. When the float valve drops down, unlock and open the lid.
8. Shred the chicken with two forks and stir everything together well.
9. Spoon into bowls and top with shredded cheese and diced avocado to serve.

Nutrition: 430 calories per serving, 8g fat, 34.9g protein, 57.5g carbs, 13.2g fiber

Navy Bean and Ham Soup

Yield: makes 8 servings

Prep Time: 10 minutes

Cook Time: 30 minutes

In the Pot Time: 50 minutes

Total Time: 1 hour

Function Buttons: Sauté, Bean/Chili

Ingredients:

- 2 tablespoons butter
- 1 large yellow onion, chopped
- 3 cloves minced garlic
- 2 large carrots, peeled and chopped
- 2 large stalks celery, peeled and chopped
- 2 cups chicken broth
- 1 pound navy beans, uncooked, rinsed and drained
- 2 medium Yukon gold potatoes, chopped
- 1 cup diced ham
- Salt and pepper

Instructions:

1. Press the Sauté button on the Instant Pot and wait for the display to read "hot."
2. Add the butter and let it melt then stir in the onions and garlic.
3. Sauté for 2 to 3 minutes until the onions are translucent then stir in the carrots and celery.
4. Cook for 2 minutes then stir in the chicken broth, scraping up the browned bits from the bottom of the pot.
5. Add the beans and potatoes then pour in enough water to cover the ingredients then stir in the diced ham.
6. Season with salt and pepper then stir everything together.
7. Close and lock the lid then press the Bean/Chili button and let it cook.
8. When the timer goes off, allow the steam to vent naturally for 10 minutes then switch the steam release valve to the "venting" position to Quick Release the remaining steam.
9. When the float valve drops down, unlock and open the lid.
10. Spoon the soup into bowls and serve hot.

Nutrition: 315 calories per serving, 5.6g fat, 18.2g protein, 48.8g carbs, 16.1g fiber

Broccoli Cheddar Soup

Yield: makes 4 servings

Prep Time: 5 minutes

Cook Time: 5 minutes

In the Pot Time: 30 minutes

Total Time: 35 minutes

Function Buttons: Sauté, Manual

Ingredients:

- 2 tablespoons butter
- 3 cloves minced garlic
- 1 medium head broccoli, chopped
- 2 pounds Yukon gold potato, chopped
- 4 cups chicken broth
- Salt and pepper
- 1 cup heavy cream
- ½ cup shredded cheddar cheese

Instructions:

1. Press the Sauté button on the Instant Pot and wait for the display to read "hot."
2. Add the butter and let it melt then stir in the garlic and cook for 30 seconds.
3. Stir in the broccoli, potatoes, and chicken broth then season with salt and pepper.
4. Close and lock the lid then press the Manual button and adjust the timer to 5 minutes.
5. When the timer goes off, allow the steam to vent naturally for 10 minutes then switch the steam release valve to the "venting" position to Quick Release the remaining steam.
6. When the float valve drops down, unlock and open the lid.
7. Stir in the cream and cheddar cheese then puree with an immersion blender until smooth.
8. Adjust the seasoning to taste then spoon into bowls.
9. Top with extra cheddar cheese and bacon bits to serve.

Nutrition: 340 calories per serving, 23.1g fat, 12.3g protein, 22.8g carbs, 4.4g fiber

White Bean Chicken Chili

Yield: makes 6 servings

Prep Time: 5 minutes

Cook Time: 15 minutes

In the Pot Time: 30 minutes

Total Time: 35 minutes

Function Buttons: Poultry

Ingredients:

- 1 ½ pounds boneless, skinless chicken breast halves
- 2 cups chicken broth
- 2 (15-ounce) cans white navy beans, rinsed and drained
- 1 ½ cups frozen corn
- 1 (4-ounce) can diced green chiles
- 1 tablespoon ground cumin
- ½ tablespoon chili powder
- ½ teaspoon garlic powder
- ½ teaspoon onion powder
- Salt and pepper

Instructions:

1. Place the chicken in the bottom of the Instant Pot.
2. Pour in the chicken broth, beans, corn, and chiles.
3. Stir in the cumin, chili powder, garlic powder, and onion powder then season with salt and pepper.
4. Close and lock the lid then press the Poultry button and adjust the timer to 15 minutes.
5. When the timer goes off, press the Cancel button and switch the steam release valve to the "venting" position to Quick Release the steam.
6. When the float valve drops down, unlock and open the lid.
7. Shred the chicken with two forks and adjust the seasoning to taste. Serve hot.

Nutrition: 320 calories per serving, 4.1g fat, 35.5g protein, 33.3g carbs, 9.6g fiber

Spinach and Brown Lentil Soup

Yield: makes 4 servings

Prep Time: 5 minutes

Cook Time: 10 minutes

In the Pot Time: 40 minutes

Total Time: 45 minutes

Function Buttons: Sauté, Manual

Ingredients:

- 2 tablespoons olive oil
- 1 medium red onion, diced
- 3 cloves minced garlic
- 2 teaspoons ground coriander
- ¾ teaspoon ground cinnamon
- ½ teaspoon ground turmeric
- ¼ teaspoon ground cloves
- ¼ teaspoon cardamom
- ¼ teaspoon ground nutmeg
- Pinch cayenne
- 2 cups brown lentils, rinsed and drained

- 8 cups water
- Salt and pepper
- 4 cups fresh baby spinach

Instructions:

1. Press the Sauté button on the Instant Pot and wait for the display to read "hot."
2. Add the oil then stir in the onion, garlic, and spices.
3. Sauté for 3 minutes then stir in the lentils and water.
4. Close and lock the lid then press the Manual button and adjust the timer to 10 minutes.
5. When the timer goes off, allow the steam to vent naturally and, when the float valve drops down, unlock and open the lid.
6. Stir in the spinach then season with salt and pepper to taste. Serve hot.

Nutrition: 385 calories per serving, 8.3g fat, 23.4g protein, 54.2g carbs, 10.7g fiber

Butternut Squash Beef Stew

Yield: makes 8 servings

Prep Time: 10 minutes

Cook Time: 30 minutes

In the Pot Time: 50 minutes

Total Time: 1 hour

Function Buttons: Sauté, Meat/Stew

Ingredients:

- 3 tablespoons olive oil
- 1 large yellow onion, chopped
- 2 large stalks celery, chopped
- 2 large carrots, peeled and chopped
- 2 cloves minced garlic
- 1 large tomato, chopped
- 2 tablespoons tomato paste
- Salt and pepper
- 2 pounds beef stew meat, chopped
- ¼ cup arrowroot starch
- 6 cups chopped butternut squash
- 1 teaspoon Hungarian paprika
- 1 teaspoon dried rosemary
- 1 teaspoon dried thyme
- 2 ½ cups beef broth
- ½ cup dry red wine

Instructions:

1. Press the Sauté button on the Instant Pot and wait for the display to read "hot."
2. Add the oil then stir in the onion, celery, carrots, and garlic.
3. Sauté for 3 minutes then stir in the tomatoes and tomato paste – season with salt and pepper.
4. Toss the beef with the arrowroot starch and season with salt and pepper.
5. Add the beef and the squash to the pot then stir in the remaining seasonings along with the beef broth and wine.
6. Close and lock the lid then press the Meat/Stew button and adjust the timer to 30 minutes.
7. When the timer goes off, press the Cancel button and switch the steam release valve to the "venting" position to Quick Release the steam.
8. When the float valve drops down, unlock and open the lid.
9. Stir the stew well then serve hot over steamed rice.

Nutrition: 360 calories per serving, 13g fat, 37.9g protein, 20.1g carbs, 3.9g fiber

Creamy Lobster Bisque

Yield: makes 8 servings

Prep Time: 10 minutes

Cook Time: 4 minutes

In the Pot Time: 25 minutes

Total Time: 35 minutes

Function Buttons: Sauté, Manual

Ingredients:

- 2 tablespoons butter
- 1 small yellow onion, diced
- 2 cloves minced garlic
- 2 (14-ounce) cans diced tomatoes
- 2 large carrots, peeled and diced
- 2 large stalks celery, diced
- 4 cups chicken broth
- 1 tablespoon Old Bay seasoning
- 1 teaspoon dried dill
- ½ teaspoon paprika
- Salt and pepper
- 4 (6-ounce) lobster tails
- 2 cups heavy cream
- Fresh chopped parsley

Instructions:

1. Press the Sauté button on the Instant Pot and wait for the display to read "hot."
2. Add the butter and let it melt for a minute then stir in the onions and garlic.
3. Cook for 2 to 3 minutes until the onions are translucent then stir in the tomatoes, carrots, and celery.
4. Pour in the chicken broth and stir in the Old Bay, dill, and paprika.

5. Season with salt and pepper then add the lobster tails to the Instant Pot.
6. Close and lock the lid then press the Manual button and adjust the timer to 4 minutes.
7. When the timer goes off, allow the steam to vent naturally and, when the float valve drops down, unlock and open the lid.
8. Remove the lobster tails from the pot and remove the flesh from the tails.
9. Puree the soup with an immersion blender then chop the lobster and stir it back into the pot.
10. Stir in the cream and serve hot with fresh parsley to garnish.

Nutrition: 260 calories per serving, 15.6g fat, 20.6g protein, 8.6g carbs, 2.2g fiber

Dessert Recipes

Recipes Included in this Chapter:

- Maple Apple Crisp
- Chocolate Cookie Cheesecake
- Single-Serve Lava Cakes
- Cinnamon Raisin Rice Pudding
- Lemon Blueberry Cake
- Banana Walnut Bread
- Angel Food Cake
- Spiced Apple Dumplings
- Peach Nectarine Cobbler
- Easy Coconut Flan
- Pineapple Upside Down Cake
- Decadent Chocolate Cheesecake
- Mixed Berry Cobbler
- Maple Crème Brulees

Maple Apple Crisp

Yield: makes 4 servings

Prep Time: 5 minutes

Cook Time: 8 minutes

In the Pot Time: 30 minutes

Total Time: 35 minutes

Function Buttons: Manual

Ingredients:

- 5 medium ripe apples, cored and peeled
- ½ cup water
- 1 to 2 tablespoons maple syrup
- ½ tablespoon ground cinnamon
- ½ teaspoon ground nutmeg
- ¼ cup butter
- ¾ cup old-fashioned oats
- ¼ cup all-purpose flour
- ¼ cup brown sugar, packed
- ½ teaspoon salt

Instructions:

1. Chop the apples into chunks then add them to the Instant Pot.
2. Stir in the water, maple syrup, cinnamon, and nutmeg.
3. Melt the butter then stir it into the oats, flour, brown sugar, and salt in a mixing bowl then spoon over the apples in the Instant Pot.
4. Close and lock the lid then press the Manual button and adjust the timer to 8 minutes.
5. When the timer goes off, allow the steam to vent naturally and, when the float valve drops down, unlock and open the lid.
6. Spoon into bowls and serve with ice cream or whipped cream.

Nutrition: 310 calories per serving, 12.2g fat, 2g protein, 51.2g carbs, 7.6g fiber

Chocolate Cookie Cheesecake

Yield: makes 8 servings

Prep Time: 20 minutes

Cook Time: 35 minutes

In the Pot Time: 1 hour

Total Time: 1 hour 20 minutes

Function Buttons: Manual

Ingredients:

- 2 tablespoons butter, melted
- 12 chocolate sandwich cookies, crushed
- 2 (8-ounce) packages cream cheese, softened
- ½ cup white sugar
- 2 large eggs
- 1 tablespoon all-purpose flour
- ¼ cup heavy cream
- 1 tablespoon vanilla extract
- 8 sandwich cookies, chopped

Instructions:

1. Grease the inside of a 7-inch spring-form pan with cooking spray and wrap the bottom tightly with foil.
2. Stir the melted butter into the crushed cookies then press the mixture into the bottom and part way up the sides of the spring-form pan.
3. Freeze for 15 minutes while you prepare the filling.
4. Beat the cream cheese in a mixing bowl until smooth then beat in the sugar.
5. Add the eggs one at a time, beating between each addition, then beat in the flour, heavy cream, and vanilla extract.
6. Fold in the chopped cookies then pour the filling into the crust.
7. Cover the spring-form pan with foil.
8. Pour 1 ½ cups of water into the Instant Pot then add the steamer insert and place the spring-form pan on top of it.
9. Close and lock the lid then press the Manual button and adjust the timer to 35 minutes.

10. When the timer goes off, allow the steam to vent naturally for 10 minutes then switch the steam release valve to the "venting" position to Quick Release the remaining steam.
11. When the float valve drops down, unlock and open the lid.
12. Remove the cheesecake from the pot and let it cool to room temperature.
13. Transfer the cheesecake to the fridge and chill for at least 8 hours, but ideally overnight.

Nutrition: 425 calories per serving, 30.1g fat, 7.4g protein, 33.1g carbs, 0.8g fiber

Single-Serve Lava Cakes

Yield: makes 3 servings

Prep Time: 5 minutes

Cook Time: 7 minutes

In the Pot Time: 20 minutes

Total Time: 25 minutes

Function Buttons: Manual

Ingredients:

- 1 cup water
- ¼ cup whole milk
- ¼ cup all-purpose flour
- ¼ cup sugar
- 2 tablespoons olive oil
- 1 large egg
- 1 ½ tablespoons unsweetened cocoa powder
- ½ teaspoon baking powder
- Pinch salt
- 1 tablespoon powdered sugar

Instructions:

1. Find three ramekins that will fit inside your Instant Pot and grease them with cooking spray or butter.
2. Pour the water into the pot and add the steamer insert.
3. Beat the milk, flour, sugar, olive oil, and egg in a mixing bowl.
4. Add the cocoa powder, baking powder, and salt then beat until well combined.
5. Divide the mixture among the three ramekins and place them into the pot on top of the steamer insert.
6. Close and lock the lid then press the Manual button and adjust the timer to 7 minutes.
7. When the timer goes off, press the Cancel button and switch the steam release valve to the "venting" position to Quick Release the steam.
8. When the float valve drops down, unlock and open the lid.
9. Remove the ramekins from the pot and sprinkle with powdered sugar to serve.

Nutrition: 235 calories per serving, 12.1g fat, 4.4g protein, 30.2g carbs, 1.2g fiber

Cinnamon Raisin Rice Pudding

Yield: makes 8 servings

Prep Time: 5 minutes

Cook Time: 3 minutes

In the Pot Time: 25 minutes

Total Time: 30 minutes

Function Buttons: Manual, Sauté

Ingredients:

- 1 ½ cups water
- 1 cup uncooked Arborio rice
- Pinch salt
- 1 ½ cups whole milk
- ½ cup sugar
- 2 large eggs
- ½ cup heavy cream
- ¾ cup seedless raisins
- 1 teaspoon vanilla extract

Instructions:

1. Stir together the water and rice with a pinch of salt in the Instant Pot.
2. Close and lock the lid then press the Manual button and adjust the timer to 3 minutes.
3. When the timer goes off, allow the steam to vent naturally for 10 minutes then switch the steam release valve to the "venting" position to Quick Release the remaining steam.
4. When the float valve drops down, unlock and open the lid.
5. Stir in the milk and sugar then let it rest for a minute or two.
6. Whisk the eggs together with the cream then pour into the pot while stirring.
7. Press the Sauté button and cook until the mixture starts to bubble then press the Cancel button.
8. Remove the inner pot from the Instant Pot and stir in the raisins and vanilla extract.
9. Let cool for 5 minutes then spoon into bowls and serve with a sprinkle of cinnamon.

Nutrition: 245 calories per serving, 5.7g fat, 5.2g protein, 44.6g carbs, 1.2g fiber

Lemon Blueberry Cake

Yield: makes 4 servings

Prep Time: 15 minutes

Cook Time: 30 minutes

In the Pot Time: 1 hour

Total Time: 1 hour 15 minutes

Function Buttons: Manual

Ingredients:

- 1 cup all-purpose flour
- 1 teaspoon baking powder
- ¼ teaspoon salt
- ¼ cup butter, softened
- 1/3 cup granulated sugar
- 2 tablespoons fresh lemon zest
- 1 large egg
- ½ teaspoon vanilla extract
- ¼ cup buttermilk, room temperature
- 1 cup fresh blueberries
- ¼ cup powdered sugar
- 1 to 2 tablespoons fresh lemon juice

Instructions:

1. Grease and flour a small cake pan that will fit inside your Instant Pot.
2. Whisk together the flour, baking powder, and salt in a mixing bowl then spoon 2 tablespoons of the mix into a small bowl and set aside.
3. Beat the butter, sugar, and lemon zest in a bowl until thoroughly combined then beat in the egg and vanilla extract.
4. Beat the dry mixture into the wet, a little at a time, alternating with the buttermilk and stir until well combined.
5. Toss the blueberries with the reserved flour mixture then fold into the batter.
6. Place the steamer insert in your Instant Pot and add 2/3 cup water.
7. Spoon the batter into the prepared pan and place it in the steamer rack.
8. Close and lock the lid then press the Manual button and adjust the timer to 30 minutes.
9. When the timer goes off, press the Cancel button and switch the steam release valve to the "venting" position to Quick Release.
10. When the float valve drops back down, unlock and open the lid then remove the cake pan.
11. Turn the cake out onto a serving dish and let cool while you prepare the glaze.
12. Whisk together the powdered sugar and lemon juice then drizzle over the cooled cake and slice to serve.

Nutrition: 360 calories per serving, 13.4g fat, 5.8g protein, 55.4g carbs, 2g fiber

Banana Walnut Bread

Yield: makes 8 servings

Prep Time: 10 minutes

Cook Time: 55 minutes

In the Pot Time: 1 hour 20 minutes

Total Time: 1 hour 30 minutes

Function Buttons: Manual

Ingredients:

- 1 cup white sugar
- ½ cup butter, softened
- 2 large eggs
- 3 overripe bananas, mashed
- 2 cups all-purpose flour
- 1 ½ teaspoons baking soda
- ½ teaspoon salt
- 1 cup chopped walnuts
- 1 ½ cups water

Instructions:

1. Grease a 6-cup bundt pan with coconut oil then set it aside.
2. Beat together the sugar, butter, and eggs until light and creamy, scraping down the sides of the bowl as needed.
3. Stir in the mashed bananas until well combined.
4. Whisk together the flour, baking soda, and salt in another bowl then stir it into the wet ingredients until just combined.
5. Fold in the walnuts then pour the batter into the prepared pan.
6. Pour 1 ½ cups of water into the Instant Pot then place the steamer rack inside and put the bundt pan on top of it.
7. Cover the pan with a paper towel then a layer of foil.
8. Close and lock the lid then press the Manual button and adjust the timer to 55 minutes.
9. When the timer goes off, allow the steam to vent naturally for 10 minutes then switch the steam release valve to the "venting" position to Quick Release the remaining steam.
10. When the float valve drops down, unlock and open the lid.
11. Remove the bundt pan and let the banana bread cool to room temperature.
12. Turn the bread out onto a cutting board and slice to serve.

Nutrition: 465 calories per serving, 22.4g fat, 9.2g protein, 60.6g carbs, 3.1g fiber

Angel Food Cake

Yield: makes 4 servings

Prep Time: 10 minutes

Cook Time: 22 minutes

In the Pot Time: 40 minutes

Total Time: 50 minutes

Function Buttons: Manual

Ingredients:

- 6 large egg whites
- ¾ cup white sugar
- 3 tablespoons warm water
- 1 ½ teaspoons vanilla extract
- ½ teaspoon cream of tartar

- ¼ teaspoon salt
- ½ cup all-purpose flour or cake flour

Instructions:

1. Beat the egg whites in a metal bowl until foamy, about 2 minutes, then beat in the sugar.
2. Add the water, vanilla, cream of tartar, and salt then beat until stiff peaks form, about 5 minutes.
3. Fold the flour into the egg whites ¼ cup at a time until just blended.
4. Spoon the batter into a 7-inch bundt pan then cover tightly with foil.
5. Pour the water into the Instant Pot and add the steamer rack and place the bundt pan on top.
6. Close and lock the lid then press the Manual button and adjust the timer to 22 minutes.
7. When the timer goes off, allow the steam to vent naturally for 5 minutes then switch the steam release valve to the "venting" position to Quick Release the remaining steam.
8. When the float valve drops down, unlock and open the lid.
9. Remove the pan from the pot and remove the foil.
10. Turn the pan over on a cooling rack and let it cool completely before removing the pan.

Nutrition: 230 calories per serving, 0.2g fat, 7g protein, 50.2g carbs. 0.4g fiber

Spiced Apple Dumplings

Yield: makes 8 servings

Prep Time: 10 minutes

Cook Time: 10 minutes

In the Pot Time: 40 minutes

Total Time: 50 minutes

Function Buttons: Manual, Sauté

Ingredients:

- 1 (8-ounce) can crescent rolls
- 1 large apple, cut into 8 slices
- ¼ cup butter
- ½ cup brown sugar, packed
- 1 teaspoon ground cinnamon
- ¾ teaspoon vanilla extract
- Pinch ground nutmeg
- ¾ cup apple cider

Instructions:

1. Press the Sauté button on the Instant Pot and wait for the display to read "hot."
2. Open the can of crescent rolls and separate the triangles.
3. Place one slice of apple on the wide end of each triangle and roll it up in the dough.
4. Add the butter to the Instant Pot and let it melt then press the Cancel button.
5. Stir in the brown sugar, cinnamon, vanilla, and nutmeg then place the dumplings in the pot and drizzle with apple cider.
6. Close and lock the lid then press the Manual button and adjust the timer to 10 minutes.
7. When the timer goes off, allow the steam to vent naturally and, when the float valve drops down, unlock and open the lid.

8. Spoon the dumplings into bowls and serve with ice cream.

Nutrition: 225 calories per serving, 11.8g fat, 2.2g protein, 26.8g carbs, 0.9g fiber

Peach Nectarine Cobbler

Yield: makes 6 servings

Prep Time: 10 minutes

Cook Time: 10 minutes

In the Pot Time: 35 minutes

Total Time: 45 minutes

Function Buttons: Manual

Ingredients: 2 ¼ cup baking mix

- ½ cup unsweetened almond milk
- 3 tablespoons butter, melted
- 4 tablespoons white sugar
- 1 teaspoon ground cinnamon
- 6 ripe peaches, peeled and sliced
- 6 ripe nectarines, peeled and sliced
- ½ cup brown sugar (or light brown sugar)
- 3 tablespoons cornstarch
- 1 tablespoon fresh lemon juice
- ¾ cup water

Instructions:

1. Whisk together the baking mix, milk, melted butter, white sugar, and cinnamon in a bowl then set aside.
2. Toss the peaches and nectarines with the brown sugar, cornstarch, lemon juice, and water – add extra cinnamon, if desired.
3. Spread the fruit in the Instant Pot then spoon the topping over it.
4. Close and lock the lid then press the Manual button and adjust the timer to 10 minutes.
5. When the timer goes off, allow the steam to vent naturally and, when the float valve drops down, unlock and open the lid.
6. Spoon into bowls and serve with vanilla ice cream.

Nutrition: 270 calories per serving, 6.9g fat, 3.1g protein, 53g carbs, 5g fiber

Easy Coconut Flan

Yield: makes 6 servings

Prep Time: 20 minutes

Cook Time: 9 minutes

In the Pot Time: 40 minutes

Total Time: 1 hour

Function Buttons: Manual

Ingredients:

- ½ cup superfine sugar
- 2 tablespoons water
- 1 cup unsweetened almond milk
- 1 cup heavy cream
- ¼ cup white sugar
- ½ tablespoon vanilla extract
- Pinch salt
- 3 large eggs, whisked

Instructions:

1. Combine the sugar and water in a small saucepan over medium-high heat.
2. Swirl (do not stir) occasionally until it turns a dark golden brown then divide among six small ramekins and cool.
3. Warm the milk and cream in a saucepan to steaming then whisk in the sugar, vanilla, and salt – stir until the sugar dissolves.
4. Beat the eggs in a bowl then pour a little of the warmed milk in while whisking – keep whisking and pour in the rest of the eggs.
5. Divide the mixture among the ramekins, pouring through a strainer, then cover the ramekins tightly with foil.
6. Pour ½ cup of water into the Instant Pot then add the steamer rack and place the ramekins on top.
7. Close and lock the lid then press the Manual button and adjust the timer to 9 minutes.
8. When the timer goes off, allow the steam to vent naturally and, when the float valve drops down, unlock and open the lid.
9. Remove the ramekins from the pot and cool to room temperature.
10. Transfer to the fridge and chill for at least 4 hours then serve.

Nutrition: 210 calories per serving, 10.5g fat, 3.7g protein, 26.2g carbs, 0.2g fiber

Pineapple Upside Down Cake

Yield: makes 8 servings

Prep Time: 10 minutes

Cook Time: 20 minutes

In the Pot Time: 45 minutes

Total Time: 55 minutes

Function Buttons: Manual

Ingredients:

- 2 cups water
- ¼ cup raw cane sugar
- ½ (20-ounce) can pineapple rings, drained
- 1 cup ricotta cheese
- 6 tablespoons white sugar
- 3 tablespoons olive oil

- 1 ½ teaspoons vanilla extract
- 1 cup all-purpose flour
- 2 teaspoons baking powder
- 1 teaspoon baking soda
- Pinch ground cinnamon

Instructions:

1. Pour the water into the Instant Pot and add the steamer insert.
2. Grease a 4-cup bowl (heat-proof) then line the bottom with parchment.
3. Lightly flour the bowl then sprinkle in the raw cane sugar and arrange the pineapple slices in the sugar.
4. Beat the egg together with the ricotta cheese, white sugar, olive oil, and vanilla with a fork then whisk in the flour, cinnamon, baking powder, and baking soda.
5. Pour the batter into the prepared bowl then place it on the steamer insert in the Instant Pot.
6. Close and lock the lid then press the Manual button and adjust the timer to 20 minutes.
7. When the timer goes off, allow the steam to vent naturally and, when the float valve drops down, unlock and open the lid.
8. Remove the bowl from the Instant Pot and let it cool to room temperature.
9. Turn the cake out onto a plate and slice to serve.

Nutrition: 215 calories per serving, 7.9g fat, 5.2g protein, 31.3g carbs, 0.5g fiber

Decadent Chocolate Cheesecake

Yield: makes 10 slices

Prep Time: 15 minutes

Cook Time: 25 minutes

In the Pot Time: 1 hour

Total Time: 1 hour 15 minutes

Function Buttons: Manual

Ingredients:

- 2 cups water
- 1 ¼ cups crushed chocolate cookies
- 5 tablespoons melted butter
- 2 (8-ounce) packages cream cheese, softened
- ¼ cup brown sugar, packed
- ¼ cup white sugar
- 1 large egg plus 2 yolks
- 8 ounces dark or semisweet chocolate, melted
- ¼ cup sour cream
- 1 tablespoon all-purpose flour
- 1 teaspoon vanilla extract
- Pinch salt

Instructions:

1. Line the base of a 7-inch spring-form pan with parchment then grease the pan with coconut oil and wrap the bottom with foil.
2. Pour the water into the Instant Pot then add the steamer insert.
3. Combine the chocolate cookie crumbs and melted butter in a bowl then press the mixture into the bottom of the spring-form pan.
4. Cream together the cream cheese with the brown sugar and white sugar in a mixing bowl.
5. Beat in the egg then beat in the egg yolks, scraping down the sides of the bowl as needed.
6. Whisk in the melted chocolate and sour cream then stir in the flour, vanilla, and salt.
7. Pour the filling into the crust and smooth it well.
8. Place the spring-form pan on the steamer insert in the Instant Pot – cover with a layer of foil, if desired.
9. Close and lock the lid then press the Manual button and adjust the timer to 25 minutes.
10. When the timer goes off, allow the steam to vent naturally for 15 minutes then switch the steam release valve to the "venting" position to Quick Release the remaining steam.
11. When the float valve drops down, unlock and open the lid.
12. Remove the cheesecake from the Instant Pot and cool to room temperature.
13. Chill for at least 8 hours before slicing to serve.

Nutrition: 450 calories per serving, 33.7g fat, 6.5g protein, 34.2g carbs, 2.1g fiber

Mixed Berry Cobbler

Yield: makes 6 servings

Prep Time: 45 minutes (including cooling time)

Cook Time: 15 minutes

In the Pot Time: 40 minutes

Total Time: 1 hour 25 minutes

Function Buttons: Manual

Ingredients:

- 1 ¾ cups water, divided
- 1 cup all-purpose flour
- 1 teaspoon baking powder
- ½ teaspoon ground cinnamon
- ¼ teaspoon ground nutmeg
- ¼ teaspoon salt
- 1 ½ cups white sugar, divided
- 2 large eggs
- 2 tablespoons milk
- 2 tablespoons coconut oil, melted
- 4 cups fresh mixed berries
- 1 tablespoon orange zest

Instructions:

1. Pour 1 cup water into the Instant Pot then place the steamer insert inside.
2. Whisk together the flour, baking powder, cinnamon, nutmeg, and salt with ¾ cup sugar in a mixing bowl.
3. In another bowl, whisk together the eggs, milk, and oil then stir into the dry ingredients until just combined.
4. Spread the batter in a greased 7-inch souffle dish.
5. Combine the berries with the remaining water, sugar, and orange zest in a saucepan and bring to a boil.
6. Remove from heat and pour over the batter then loosely cover the dish with foil.
7. Place the dish in the Instant Pot on the steamer rack.
8. Close and lock the lid then press the Manual button and adjust the timer to 15 minutes.
9. When the timer goes off, allow the steam to vent naturally for 10 minutes then switch the steam release valve to the "venting" position to Quick Release the remaining steam.
10. When the float valve drops down, unlock and open the lid.
11. Remove the souffle dish to a cooling rack and cool for 30 minutes.
12. Spoon the cobbler into bowls and serve with ice cream.

Nutrition: 385 calories per serving, 6.9g fat, 5.1g protein, 78.4g carbs, 4.1g fiber

Maple Crème Brulees

Yield: makes 3 servings

Prep Time: 15 minutes

Cook Time: 10 minutes

In the Pot Time: 35 minutes

Total Time: 50 minutes

Function Buttons: Sauté (Less), Manual

Ingredients:

- 1 ¼ cup heavy cream
- 3 large egg yolks
- ½ cup brown sugar, packed
- ½ teaspoon ground cinnamon
- ½ teaspoon maple extract
- 1 cup water
- 3 teaspoons cane sugar

Instructions:

1. Press the Sauté button on the Instant Pot and adjust it to Less.
2. Pour in the cream and heat until it just starts to bubble.
3. Meanwhile, whisk together the egg yolks, brown sugar, and cinnamon.
4. When the cream is bubbling, press the Cancel button then stir a little of the egg yolk mixture into the pot.
5. Pour in the rest, stirring constantly, then stir in the maple extract.

6. Divide the mixture among three greased 6-ounce ramekins then clean the inner pot and pour in 1 cup of water.
7. Place the steamer insert in the pot and place the ramekins on top and cover loosely with foil.
8. Close and lock the lid then press the Manual button and adjust the timer to 10 minutes.
9. When the timer goes off, allow the steam to vent naturally for 10 minutes then switch the steam release valve to the "venting" position to Quick Release the remaining steam.
10. When the float valve drops down, unlock and open the lid.
11. Remove the ramekins from the pot and cool on a cooling rack for 10 minutes.
12. Transfer to the refrigerator and chill, covered, for at least 4 hours.
13. Sprinkle the cane sugar over the ramekins and melt with a blow torch to caramelize then serve immediately.

Nutrition: 340 calories per serving, 23g fat, 3.8g protein, 30.1g carbs, 0.2g fiber

Conclusion

Congratulations! You've made it through the entire cookbook and are now well equipped to take the culinary world by storm! Okay, maybe that might be a little exaggerated, but not by much!

By now, you should have a thorough understanding of what your Instant Pot has to offer and you're ready to start using it to prepare healthy, homemade meals for yourself and your family. Not only is the Instant Pot easy to use, but it does the work of half a dozen kitchen appliances all in one!

So, you've learned how to assemble your Instant Pot and how to use all of the preset buttons. You've learned how to do a Natural Release and how to do a Quick Release. You've also learned how to use all of the extras that come with the device to make your favorite dishes in half the time (or less) than cooking on the stovetop. What else could you possibly need?

Before letting you go, I want to give you a few quick and easy tips for getting the most out of your Instant Pot. Here they are:

- Always use at least ½ to 1 cup of liquid when pressure cooking – liquid is required to pressurize the unit so, if you don't use enough, it won't work.
- You can use the Sauté function to sauté or stir-fry ingredients without using the ½ cup of liquid – use the Instant Pot like you would use a regular frying pan on the stovetop and adjust the heat using the Less and More buttons.
- Remember that you can adjust the time and pressure for all of the preset buttons using the (-)/(+) buttons – you can also use them to adjust the Manual setting.
- Know that it will take 10 to 15 minutes for the Instant Pot to pressurize when you are using the pressure cooking function – this time is accounted for in the "In the Pot Time" for each recipe.
- Always check the steam pressure valve before starting the timer – if you are pressure cooking, it needs to be in the "sealing" rather than the "venting" position or the pot won't come to pressure.
- Never open the Instant Pot when it is coming to pressure – it will be very difficult to open the pot during pressurization but if you do it you'll be hit in the face with a blast of hot steam.
- Buy some extras of the things you use most such as the sealing ring and the inner pot – having more than one of these on hand ensures that if something happens to one, you'll still be able to use your Instant Pot.

With these helpful tips in mind and the rest of the information provided in this book, you are well on your way to becoming an Instant Pot master. Best of luck and have fun using your Instant Pot!

About The Author

A person who loves to cook, Laurel embarked on her culinary journey when she was just a wee one in the homey kitchen of her grandma. Those were among the most formative years of her life and that is where she learnt how to cook.

She took it a step further and traversed the world, learning and cooking different cuisines with wide eyed wonder and child-like curiosity.

This book is one of the results of her constant search for great food at a budget without having too complicated prepping steps to boot!

Made in the USA
Columbia, SC
25 September 2018